Introduction to Zoning and Development Regulation

Fourth Edition 2013

David W. Owens

UNC
SCHOOL OF
GOVERNMENT

The School of Government at the University of North Carolina at Chapel Hill works to improve the lives of North Carolinians by engaging in practical scholarship that helps public officials and citizens understand and improve state and local government. Established in 1931 as the Institute of Government, the School provides educational, advisory, and research services for state and local governments. The School of Government is also home to a nationally ranked graduate program in public administration and specialized centers focused on information technology and environmental finance.

As the largest university-based local government training, advisory, and research organization in the United States, the School of Government offers up to 200 courses, webinars, and specialized conferences for more than 12,000 public officials each year. In addition, faculty members annually publish approximately 50 books, manuals, reports, articles, bulletins, and other print and online content related to state and local government. Each day that the General Assembly is in session, the School produces the *Daily Bulletin Online*, which reports on the day's activities for members of the legislature and others who need to follow the course of legislation.

The Master of Public Administration Program is offered in two formats. The full-time, two-year residential program serves up to 60 students annually. In 2013 the School launched MPA@UNC, an online format designed for working professionals and others seeking flexibility while advancing their careers in public service. The School's MPA program consistently ranks among the best public administration graduate programs in the country, particularly in city management. With courses ranging from public policy analysis to ethics and management, the program educates leaders for local, state, and federal governments and nonprofit organizations.

Operating support for the School of Government's programs and activities comes from many sources, including state appropriations, local government membership dues, private contributions, publication sales, course fees, and service contracts. Visit www.sog.unc.edu or call 919.966.5381 for more information on the School's courses, publications, programs, and services.

Michael R. Smith, DEAN
Thomas H. Thornburg, SENIOR ASSOCIATE DEAN
Frayda S. Bluestein, ASSOCIATE DEAN FOR FACULTY DEVELOPMENT
L. Ellen Bradley, ASSOCIATE DEAN FOR PROGRAMS AND MARKETING
Todd A. Nicolet, ASSOCIATE DEAN FOR OPERATIONS
Bradley G. Volk, ASSOCIATE DEAN FOR ADMINISTRATION

FACULTY

Whitney Afonso	James C. Drennan	Adam Lovelady	Dale J. Roenigk
Trey Allen	Richard D. Ducker	James M. Markham	John Rubin
Gregory S. Allison	Joseph S. Ferrell	Christopher B. McLaughlin	Jessica Smith
David N. Ammons	Alyson A. Grine	Kara A. Millonzi	Meredith Smith
Ann M. Anderson	Norma Houston	Jill D. Moore	Carl W. Stenberg III
A. Fleming Bell, II	Cheryl Daniels Howell	Jonathan Q. Morgan	John B. Stephens
Maureen Berner	Jeffrey A. Hughes	Ricardo S. Morse	Charles Szypszak
Mark F. Botts	Willow S. Jacobson	C. Tyler Mulligan	Shannon H. Tufts
Michael Crowell	Robert P. Joyce	Kimberly L. Nelson	Vaughn Mamlin Upshaw
Leisha DeHart-Davis	Kenneth L. Joyner	David W. Owens	Aimee N. Wall
Shea Riggsbee Denning	Diane M. Juffras	LaToya B. Powell	Jeffrey B. Welty
Sara DePasquale	Dona G. Lewandowski	William C. Rivenbark	Richard B. Whisnant

Printed in the United States of America
21 20 19 18 17 3 4 5 6 7
ISBN 978-1-56011-744-5

Contents

Introduction

Land use and development decisions generate tremendous public interest, making zoning one of the most visible and important functions of local governments. Indeed, few local government issues will pack a hearing room more quickly than a controversial zoning case:

- Should multifamily or commercial development be allowed on this site?
- Will this rezoning increase traffic congestion or lead to overcrowded schools?
- Is there any way we can protect this historic neighborhood or these natural resources if this development is approved?
- Will this zoning decision stifle economic development?
- What will this do to my property values?

The issues involved affect the public directly and substantially. It is not surprising that citizens are intensely interested and pressure local governments to "get it right" when making zoning decisions, especially when the issue at hand affects their property or neighborhood.

Many critical zoning decisions are made by citizens serving on government panels rather than by professionally trained local government staff. City council members and county commissioners, for example, decide whether to rezone a parcel of land. Board of adjustment members decide whether to grant a variance to zoning regulations. Planning board members advise on rezonings and may make final decisions on special approvals required for some developments. These decisions can have a tremendous impact on landowners, their neighbors, and the future quality of the entire community. Both the citizen board members making these decisions and the citizens attempting to influence the choices must fully understand the legal requirements for zoning in order to do their jobs fairly and effectively.

This book is intended to provide a clear, understandable explanation of zoning for citizen board members and the public. It is not a detailed legal treatise on zoning law; rather, it is an introduction for citizens new to these issues or a refresher for those who have been at the zoning business for some time. Those who need more detailed information may check the notes cited at the end of many chapters or the more detailed books and reports listed in the Appendix.

Each chapter of this book deals with a distinct aspect of zoning and development regulation. The book can be read in its entirety, or the reader can turn to a question of particular interest. The table of contents or the index will give the reader quick directions to topics of interest. In addition, a glossary of zoning terms is included at the end of the book.

This book also contains occasional brief sections that examine landmark North Carolina zoning cases and the human dimension of zoning in more detail. These sections are shaded in order to distinguish them from the regular text.

Many aspects of law and practice are similar throughout the country. However, each state's law has its nuances and peculiarities. This book is based on zoning and development regulation by North Carolina cities and counties. Readers in other states are cautioned not to assume that everything addressed here is directly applicable elsewhere—much of it is, but there are often subtle yet important differences from state to state.

Chapter 1

Fundamentals

Americans have always cherished personal freedom and independence. Anyone involved with zoning and development regulation very long has been confronted with the challenge, "This land has been in my family for generations. I'll do with it as I please. Government has no right telling me what I can and cannot do on my own land." Yet in spite of this widely held sentiment, zoning and other development ordinances are among the most common regulations adopted by local governments. Why do we so often choose to subject ourselves and our neighbors to this government regulation?

As North Carolina's woods, farms, and small villages of fifty years ago made way for cities, suburbs, industrial parks, and shopping malls, communities have had to adjust to the change. Citizens find themselves wrestling with difficult questions. They ask, Is this the kind of place I want to live, where my children will want to live? How can we encourage quality growth and development while keeping the things that make our community a special place? How can we embrace the positive aspects of change and avoid the negative aspects?

Some of these questions about growth and community transitions address the big picture: How can we provide safe, decent, and affordable housing for all citizens? How can we protect the quality of our air, our water, and natural resources? How can we make our cities attractive, efficient, and livable? Other questions are much more immediate and personal: What will the new strip development along the bypass do to my business downtown?

How will a fast food place on the corner affect my neighborhood? Can I put a mobile home out behind the home place so I can care for my ailing mother?

Because the way one person uses his or her land can so deeply affect neighbors and the broader community, it is not surprising that the role of government in addressing these questions has grown. Local governments undertake a variety of activities to address the questions noted above. They prepare plans and conduct studies to better understand the implications of such decisions. Citizens talk about the directions they want their community to take. And communities adopt regulations that limit what people can do with their land.

Land use regulations are often adopted to assure that one person does not use his or her land in a way that will harm neighbors or the community. These regulations, while adopted to benefit everyone by promoting the common good, do limit our personal choices. Finding the right balance of individual and community interests is a demanding job, one fraught with controversy, difficult choices, and a host of legal rules.

While local governments use many tools for land use planning and regulation, the principal tool for land use regulation in North Carolina and across the country is zoning. Other development regulations, such as subdivision regulations, are also frequently used. Increasingly a number of different development regulations are combined into a single ordinance, often termed a "unified development ordinance" or "land use management ordinance," or something similar. Almost all urban areas and many rural counties in the United States have adopted ordinances to regulate how land is used and developed.

Property owners in a residential neighborhood rely on local zoning ordinances to protect the economic value of their homes and the family character of their neighborhood. Owners of vacant land rely on zoning to determine what they can build and sell there, a decision that often has a substantial impact on the value of the land. Those financing home buyers and business development rely on zoning to provide stability and predictability in real estate markets.

Local governments also use development regulations to project what kinds of urban services, such as roads, water and sewer lines, and schools, will be needed, as well as when and where they need to be installed. The cost of providing these services affects the taxes everyone pays. Planning ahead by using these regulations can help keep costs and taxes under control.

Zoning can be used to separate incompatible uses of land, preserve the character of neighborhoods, protect natural resources, or promote economic development. Indeed, the emergence of zoning as the principal way we collectively deal with issues of land use and development led U.S. Supreme Court Justice Thurgood Marshall to note in a 1974 case that zoning "may indeed be the most essential function performed by local government, for it is one of the primary means by which we protect that sometimes difficult to define concept of quality of life."[1]

Zoning Basics

The basic principle of zoning is simple: zoning creates a number of different districts, or "zones," in a city or county, each of which sets specific rules on how the land in that district can be used. For example, a district set aside for residential land uses may exclude businesses and industries. A local governing body sets forth the specific rules and zone boundaries in the form of a zoning ordinance. Other aspects of development regulations address more specific topics, such as land subdivision.

Zoning ordinances, in addition to specifying land uses permitted in each zone, often also set detailed standards on how permitted uses may be carried out. For example, zoning ordinances often include instructions on "setbacks," the minimum distances new buildings should be set back from the street, property lines, or a stream. Other kinds of requirements, or "development standards," commonly found in zoning ordinances include the minimum number of parking spaces businesses must have for their customers, the maximum size of advertising signs, standard lot sizes or building heights, and landscaping requirements.

Virtually all zoning decisions are made by local governments, both in North Carolina and nationally. Technically, however, zoning power is a state government power that has been delegated to cities and counties. This is significant because it means that the state legislature passes laws that set the legal framework within which local governments adopt, amend, and implement their zoning and other development regulations. State statutes "enable" or authorize local governments to adopt these ordinances. While local governments decide whether to have zoning and what the content of the ordinance will be, the process they must follow in making those decisions is set by state law. The state legislature imposes a number of special requirements on how these powers may be exercised. These statutes ensure that the ordinance adoption process includes broad public notice and discussion of the policies and standards proposed. The courts also impose legal limits, mostly by protecting the due process rights of persons affected by regulatory decisions.

Given the importance of development regulation and its impacts on land-owners, neighbors, and the community, it is not surprising that a substantial body of law has developed detailing how zoning is carried out. The chapters that follow discuss these legal requirements and restrictions on development regulation.

Actors in the Process

A number of different local government bodies participate in the zoning and development regulation process. The city council or county board of commissioners, the planning board, and the board of adjustment all play key roles. In addition, local government planning and zoning staff provide essential support in zoning administration and enforcement. While some states provide for state agency oversight of some aspects of this work, in North Carolina these decisions are left to cities and counties without state or regional supervision.

North Carolina law gives each local government considerable flexibility in determining how to allocate regulatory decisions to various boards and agencies; the three boards described below commonly take charge of major aspects of development regulation. Smaller towns often combine several of these boards into a single board.

Governing board. The local governing board—the city council or county board of commissioners—controls local zoning and development regulation. This governing board makes final policy decisions. It decides whether or not to have zoning, determines what land uses are allowed in each zone, and sets the rules for development. The governing board amends the ordinance as needed and appoints the members of the other citizen boards involved. The governing board is responsible for adopting a zoning system that fits the needs of the individual community. Therefore the governing board should first understand and approve the policies that serve as the foundation for development regulation and then conduct ongoing reviews of the system to ensure it is working as intended.

Planning board. The planning board or planning commission is a group of citizens who provide advice to the governing board on planning and regulatory issues. The planning board can be of any size (it must have at least three members) and may be constituted however the governing board deems appropriate. Many cities and counties seek out active community leaders for planning board service. Often they will seek to have various points of view and various neighborhoods represented. The governing board must appoint a planning board before adopting a zoning ordinance.

Cities and counties must refer all proposed zoning amendments to the planning board for review. Some governing boards also assign to their planning boards either advisory or final decision-making authority for special and conditional use permits. Planning boards may help with a number of other matters, such as development of a comprehensive plan, community and economic development programs, plat reviews under a subdivision ordinance, and the like. The governing board may also assign to the planning board any or all of the functions of a board of adjustment.

Board of adjustment. The board of adjustment is rarely involved in setting policies. Rather, this board interprets and applies the standards that have been placed in the zoning ordinance by the governing board. The governing board appoints at least five members to this board. Each member must have a set, three-year term. The board may also have alternate members who participate in the place of an absent member or a member who must not participate in an individual case due to a conflict of interest. The board of adjustment hears individual quasi-judicial cases, such as appeals; requests for special or conditional use permits; and variance petitions. The statutes require a four-fifths vote of the board of adjustment to issue a variance. Decisions of this board are appealed directly to the courts.

Table 1.1 illustrates a typical allocation of responsibilities among these groups.

Staff. City or county managers hire the staff members who administer development regulations. Staff in the planning department, inspections department, and manager's office provide support to the process, preparing drafts of ordinances, processing permits, enforcing ordinances, and keeping the records of the citizen boards. In a few instances in North Carolina, the planning staff is hired directly by the planning board. Local governments

Table 1.1 Local Government Planning and Development Regulation Functions

Agency	Primary role	Other possibilities
Governing board (city council, county board of commissioners)	Legislative decisions: adopts ordinances, amendments, policy statements, budgets; approves acquisitions; makes appointments to other bodies	May also serve as planning agency; may approve plats and special use permits
Planning board (planning board; planning commission; planning committee of governing board)	Advisory decisions: sponsors planning studies; recommends policies, advises governing board; coordinates public participation; must recommend initial zoning ordinance and comment on all amendments	May also serve as board of adjustment; may approve or review plats
Board of adjustment	Quasi-judicial decisions: hears zoning appeals, petitions for variances, and sometimes requests for special and conditional use permits	
Staff (planning department, inspections department, community development department)	Administrative decisions: issues permits, conducts technical studies, initiates enforcement; advises manager; provides staff support for elected and appointed boards	

can also secure staff assistance in zoning from private consultants, from the state Division of Community Assistance, or from regional planning agencies.

Others. There are a number of other entities that may play some role in development regulation. A historic preservation commission, for example, may review permits related to specially designated historic districts or landmarks. Locally appointed community appearance commissions and economic development commissions rarely work directly in regulatory implementation, but their activities may need to be closely coordinated with zoning and development regulation.

Types of Decisions

The legal rules for how zoning decisions are made vary significantly depending upon the type of zoning decision involved. Zoning decisions can be grouped into four categories: legislative, quasi-judicial, advisory, and administrative. Often the body charged with making the decision varies according to the type of decision involved. Governing boards usually make legislative decisions but can also make quasi-judicial decisions. Planning boards usually make advisory decisions but can also make quasi-judicial decisions. The rules that must be followed change depending on the type of decision involved, and these rules apply no matter which board is making the decision. Therefore, knowing the type of decision is vital to determining what decision-making process should be used.

Legislative decisions affect the entire community by setting the policies and standards included in ordinances. They include decisions to adopt, amend, or repeal zoning and other ordinances. The zoning map is a part of the zoning ordinance, so amending the map to rezone even an individual parcel of land is a legislative decision. Because legislative decisions have such an important impact on landowners, neighbors, and the public, state law mandates public notice and hearing requirements. Broad public discussion and careful deliberation are encouraged, and substantial discretion in these decisions is allowed. These decisions are made by the local governing board, which "legislates" or sets policy. This body is either the city council or county board of commissioners. The state legislature does not usually make or review these decisions (though the General Assembly has the legal authority to do so and on occasion does).

Quasi-judicial decisions involve the application of policies to individual situations. Examples include variances, special and conditional use permits (even if issued by the governing board), appeals, and interpretations. These decisions involve two key elements—the finding of facts regarding the specific proposal and the exercise of judgment and discretion in applying predetermined policies to the situation. Since quasi-judicial decisions do not involve setting new policies, the broad public notice requirements that exist for legislative decisions do not apply. However, the courts have imposed fairly strict procedural requirements on these decisions in order to protect the legal rights of the parties involved. Quasi-judicial decisions are most often assigned to boards of adjustment, appointed by the governing board. But some or all of these decisions can also be assigned to the planning board or to the governing board itself.

Advisory decisions are made by bodies that may recommend decisions on a matter but have no final decision-making authority over it. The most common example is the advice on rezoning petitions given by planning boards to the city council or board of county commissioners. Advisory review is sometimes mandated by the state in order to secure additional public review of proposed zoning policy choices. There are no special rules set by state law or by the courts on how advisory decisions are made, so there is little further discussion of advisory decisions in this book. Such decisions can, however, provide thoughtful review and commentary on proposed policies. The absence of further discussion about them here reflects more the lack of special rules or restrictions placed on them than any lack of importance of advisory comments.

Administrative decisions (also known as "ministerial" decisions) are typically made by professional staff in various government departments. Such decisions cover the day-to-day nondiscretionary matters related to the implementation of ordinances, including issuing basic permits, interpreting the ordinance, and enforcing it. Administrative decisions involve the application of objective standards, such as the application of specified height limits and property line setbacks. Examples include issuing a certificate of zoning compliance for a permitted use or a notice of violation. These decisions may be appealed to the board of adjustment. If the standards to be applied require judgment, such as whether a proposed project is "compatible" with the surrounding neighborhood, the decision is quasi-judicial.

Hearings

Before a land use regulatory decision is made, it is often useful and sometimes legally necessary to gather information and public comment. This is particularly the case with zoning decisions. State law requires that a formal hearing be conducted prior to making either legislative or quasi-judicial zoning decisions. No hearings are required for advisory or administrative zoning decisions.

Since the forums for soliciting information for both legislative and quasi-judicial decisions are typically called "hearings," many people mistakenly believe that hearings for the two kinds of decisions are conducted in the same way. This is not the case, though citizens and board members accustomed to one type of hearing may well not realize they have to follow an entirely different set of ground rules when attending a hearing on a different type of decision. Careful attention to the type of decision involved is necessary to prevent use of the wrong set of procedures.

Legislative hearings are required prior to making legislative decisions. The purpose of these hearings is to gather opinions on a proposed policy. They are formal mechanisms to secure citizens' comments on a specific proposal. These are often called public hearings. They must be conducted in a fair, orderly manner to allow citizen opinion to be expressed directly to those making policy decisions. Public hearings must be held by the governing board (and additional hearings may be held by the planning board or other advisory bodies). State law requires newspaper notice of all hearings on amendments to development regulations and also requires individual mailed and posted notice when a rezoning (a zoning map amendment) is involved. Speakers are not placed under oath and the board need not make formal findings at the conclusion of the hearing. Reasonable time limits can be placed on speakers and on the overall length of the hearing.

Evidentiary hearings are used in making quasi-judicial decisions. The purpose of these hearings is to gather evidence in deciding an individual case. They are more like court proceedings than the usual public hearing on a rezoning. These hearings are required for variances, special and conditional use permits, and appeals of the staff's formal ordinance interpretations. The purpose of an evidentiary hearing is to gather facts, not to solicit citizen opinions. In these hearings, witnesses present testimony under oath and are subject to cross-examination, exhibits are submitted, detailed minutes are kept, and a formal written decision is rendered by the body holding the hearing. These legal requirements apply to any board assigned the responsibility for making quasi-judicial decisions, be it the governing board, planning board, or board of adjustment.

Table 1.2 summarizes some of the key differences between legislative public hearings and evidentiary hearings.

In addition to these two types of formal hearings, many local governments often also conduct more informal public meetings to inform the public about a pending matter and solicit comments. Such forums are most often used for advisory decisions or as a prelude to a legislative hearing. They are not mandated by state law, and they may be conducted in any manner the city or county deems appropriate.

Table 1.2 Some Key Differences between Legislative and Quasi-Judicial Decisions

	Legislative	Quasi-judicial
Decision-maker	Only governing board can decide (others may advise)	Can be board of adjustment, planning board, or governing board
Notice of hearing	Newspaper notice, plus mailed and posted notice to owners and neighbors required for zoning map amendments (and actual notice to owner for third party rezonings)	Only mailed notice to parties and posting of site required unless ordinance mandates otherwise
Type of hearing	Legislative	Evidentiary
Speakers at hearing	Can reasonably limit number of speakers, time for speakers	Witnesses are presenting testimony and are limited to relevant evidence that is not repetitious
Evidence	None required; members free to discuss issue outside of hearing	Must have substantial, competent, material evidence in record; witnesses under oath, subject to cross-examination; no ex parte communication allowed
Findings	None required, but must adopt brief statement on rationale for zoning amendments	Written decision required that includes determination of contested facts and application to applicable standards
Voting	Simple majority, but three-fourths required if protest petition filed on city rezoning	Four-fifths majority for variances; simple majority otherwise
Standard for decision	Sets standard	Can only apply standards previously set in ordinance
Conditions	Not allowed (unless included within conditional zoning)	Allowed if based on standard in ordinance
Time to initiate judicial review	Two months to file challenge to rezoning; one year for others	30 days to file challenge
Conflict of interest	Requires direct, substantial financial interest to disqualify	Any financial interest or personal bias disqualifies
Creation of vested right	None	Yes, if substantial expenditures are made in reliance on it

Public Access to Meetings and Records

In North Carolina, as in many states, the law requires most public meetings and records be open to the public.

Whenever a majority of the members of any public board (and any committee of a board) meet to discuss business, advance notice of the meeting must be provided, full and accurate minutes of the meeting must be kept, and the public must be allowed to observe the meeting.[2] There are some very limited instances where a board is allowed to conduct closed sessions, such as when the board is getting advice from its attorney on a pending lawsuit or when the board is conducting a personnel evaluation of one of its staff members. It is rare that a land use regulatory matter will qualify for discussion in a closed session. Open public meetings are required for everything from a planning board workshop on a rezoning proposal to a board of adjustment deliberation on a variance petition. A meeting of professional staff members to discuss a regulatory matter is not required to be open to the public.

All documents, reports, and letters sent or received in the course of business are considered public records, including staff reports presented to the citizen boards, minutes of meetings, and staff logs of complaints received.[3] These records must be made available for public inspection at reasonable times in the offices where the records are normally kept. A reasonable fee can be charged for copying these materials.

Notes

1. Village of Belle Terre v. Boraas, 416 U.S. 1, 13 (1974) (Marshall, J., dissenting).
2. DAVID M. LAWRENCE, OPEN MEETINGS AND LOCAL GOVERNMENTS IN NORTH CAROLINA (7th ed. 2008).
3. DAVID M. LAWRENCE, PUBLIC RECORDS LAW FOR NORTH CAROLINA LOCAL GOVERNMENTS (2nd ed. 2009).

Chapter 2

City and County Jurisdiction

Which unit of government has authority to regulate development in a particular geographic area?

Zoning and other development regulations are state powers delegated to local governments. The state legislature sets the rules for which local government can exercise these powers and where that can be done. This authority could be assigned to local governments, a state agency, multi-county councils of government, or special agencies covering metropolitan regions. The choice that has been made in North Carolina, as in most states, is to assign zoning and similar development regulations almost exclusively to cities and counties.

As for the division of responsibility between cities and counties, the general rule is that city development regulations apply to land inside the city limits and county development regulations apply outside of city limits. Property is subject to either city or county development regulation; there are no situations where both apply. For example, while Mecklenburg County is the state's most populous county, that county government has very little zoning jurisdiction because almost all of the land within the county is covered by city zoning (that is, by Charlotte and the six other municipalities within Mecklenburg County).

There are, however, two important variations on the general rule. First, North Carolina cities have authority to extend their development regulations to the urban fringe area just outside of the city limits. This is called municipal extraterritorial jurisdiction. Second, cities and counties can agree to vary these standard arrangements by individual interlocal agreements. For example, a small city may ask a county to exercise county zoning within that city.

City Jurisdiction

Cities have exclusive authority to adopt, amend, and repeal development regulations within their city limits. When a city adopts a particular development regulation, it must apply it to all the land within its boundaries. Unlike counties, cities do not have the option of zoning only a part of their jurisdiction.

City boundaries change. When a city grows, it can absorb newly developing areas just outside its borders. This expansion of the city's boundaries is called annexation. In North Carolina, the state statutes have very detailed standards for when a city can expand through annexation. Annexation can be done at the request of the landowners. This is often called "voluntary annexation." In the past, North Carolina cities also routinely annexed surrounding lands once they developed to urban densities whether or not the residents there wanted to be annexed. Annexations initiated by cities rather than landowners—often called "involuntary annexations"—are less common now, as they require a referendum and can only occur if a majority of the voters in the affected area approve.

When the city does expand its boundaries, it must amend its zoning map to extend its zoning to the newly annexed land. A transition provision in the statutes allows any county zoning that was in place prior to annexation to remain in effect for up to sixty days after the annexation becomes effective while the city holds the required hearings to amend its zoning ordinance. However, the county zoning automatically expires when the city adopts zoning for that area. If the city has not acted within sixty days from the day the area became part of the city, the county zoning expires even if the city has not yet zoned the area. Cities can start the notice and hearing process on the zoning amendment before the effective date of the annexation if they want the change in jurisdiction and the application of city zoning to happen simultaneously.

County Jurisdiction

In 1959, counties in North Carolina were given general authority to adopt zoning. Before then, only a few of the larger, more urbanized counties had gotten special authority to adopt zoning, and zoning in North Carolina was largely confined to cities. Most counties have now adopted some degree of zoning, subdivision ordinances, and other development regulations as well.

County governments in North Carolina have the option of zoning only a portion of their jurisdictions. A county can zone all of the non-city territory in the county or only a part of the county, or it can choose to have no zoning at all.

If the county chooses to zone only part of its jurisdiction, each area zoned must be at least 640 acres (one square mile) and must contain at least ten tracts of land in separate ownership. Counties may later add smaller contiguous acreages to a zoned area. A county can have multiple zoned areas, but each must meet the 640-acre threshold. If a county elects to zone only a portion of its unincorporated area, it can elect to apply its subdivision ordinance only to the zoned portions or to the entire unincorporated area.

See the map in Figure 2.1 showing which counties have adopted zoning.

City Extraterritorial Jurisdiction

The manner in which an area immediately outside a city is developed can dramatically affect the city. Development can change the character of neighborhoods, increase the demand for city services, change the city's traffic patterns, and affect surrounding property values. In many instances nearby areas may eventually become a part of the city.

As zoning and other land use regulations first came into widespread use in North Carolina, planning and development regulation were almost exclusively municipal concerns. Most cities of any size had adopted zoning by the late 1940s. By contrast, a handful of urban counties had gotten individual approval to adopt zoning, but most counties in the state had no authority to adopt zoning ordinances until 1959. As the post–World War II development boom took off, a good deal of that development occurred along the urban fringe, often in unregulated areas just outside of city corporate limits. In 1953 the Institute of Government's land use law expert, Phil Green, observed that most of this fringe area development was taking place in "relatively chaotic fashion." To deal with this unregulated development on the urban

Figure 2.1   Adoption of Zoning by North Carolina Counties

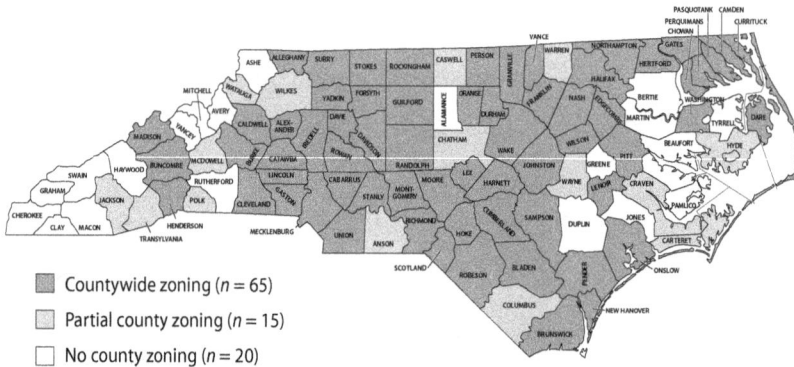

- Countywide zoning (n = 65)
- Partial county zoning (n = 15)
- No county zoning (n = 20)

Most of the state's counties now apply zoning outside of cities.

fringe, several cities in the late 1940s and early 1950s obtained legislative approval to adopt "perimeter zoning."

The Municipal Government Study Commission examined the issue in 1958 and came to this conclusion:

> The Commission recognizes that municipalities have a special interest in the areas immediately adjacent to their limits. These areas, in the normal course of events, will at some time be annexed to the city, bringing with them any problems growing out of chaotic and disorganized development. Even prior to that time they affect the city. Health and safety problems arising outside the city do not always respect city limits as they spread. . . . Subdividers of land outside the city commonly wish to tie to city water and sewerage systems. New industrial and commercial development may, for a variety of reasons, take place just outside the corporate limits.[1]

The study recommended that cities be granted an area of extraterritorial jurisdiction for land use planning and development regulation. The legislature granted statewide authority for municipal extraterritorial land use regulation in 1959. The current statutory scheme of tiered extraterritorial jurisdiction of one to three miles based on city population was adopted in 1971.

This area adjacent to cities where city land development regulations can be applied is called a city's extraterritorial jurisdiction, commonly referred

Table 2.1   Powers Allocated to Cities in the ETJ

Regulations

Zoning

Subdivision

Historic districts and landmarks

Development agreements

Construction of wireless telecommunication facilities

Building inspection

Minimum housing codes

Erosion and sedimentation control

Floodway regulation

Mountain ridge protection

Transportation corridor official maps

Regulation of forestry activities

Stormwater control ordinances (and nonregulatory aspects of stormwater management systems)

Planning, Grants, and Development Programs

Planning

Acquisition of open space

Community appearance commissions

Community development grants and programs

Acquisition and disposition of property for redevelopment

Urban Development Action Grants and urban homesteading programs

Downtown development projects

Financing renewable energy and energy efficiency programs

to as the ETJ. The extraterritorial area need not meet the same standards that are required for annexation in order to be included in a city's zoning ordinance.

Within the ETJ area, the city can prepare land use plans and apply all of its land use ordinances—zoning, subdivision, floodway, and sedimentation control ordinances as well as building and housing codes. Cities can also acquire open space and apply their community development and community beautification programs in an ETJ. Table 2.1 lists the powers that shift from the county to the city upon adoption of an ETJ area.

Within the ETJ, the city has exclusive jurisdiction for planning and development regulation. A city may not apply an ordinance in the ETJ that it is not also applying within the city, but it is not required to apply all city development ordinances that apply in the city to the ETJ. The county may apply county development regulations within an ETJ only if formally requested to do so by the city council and only if the county board of commissioners agrees to do so.

Establishment of an ETJ does not affect jurisdiction for ordinances that are not development regulations. These regulations are often referred to as "general police power" ordinances. These include both general regulations to protect the health, safety, or welfare of citizens as well as a variety of specific ordinances (regulations on abandoned and junk cars, public health nuisances, flea markets, places of amusement, outdoor advertising, solar collectors, disposal of trash, garbage and solid wastes, and parking areas). All of these general police power regulations may be applied by the county—but not by cities—within an ETJ. The only exceptions to this limit are that these city ordinances can be applied on city-owned property outside the city and that ordinances regulating swimming, surfing, littering, and personal watercraft can be applied by some cities to waterways in their ETJs.

The maximum size of an extraterritorial area depends on a city's population. The larger the population, the larger the ETJ may be, with a maximum boundary of three miles outside the city limits. (See Table 2.2.) The population figures used are the state's annual official estimates of municipal population. The maximum ETJ limits are measured from a city's principal boundaries. A city cannot extend its ETJ to the fringe area around any non-contiguous areas of the city (its satellite annexations). Land used for farming is exempt from city ETJ while the land is in active farm use.

A city can choose to exercise less than its maximum extraterritorial area. For example, it may establish jurisdiction extending one mile east of town because that is the direction of urban growth, while not establishing any extraterritorial jurisdiction on the west side of town. Figure 2.2 illustrates this sort of arrangement. If two cities are close enough together that their extraterritorial boundaries overlap, the boundary is set at the midpoint between the cities. (See Figure 2.3.) Cities that are close to each other also have the option of mutually agreeing to some other division of authority.

State law encourages cities to use identifiable geographic features, such as rivers, roads, or rail lines, when setting the actual boundaries of extraterritorial areas. The boundary need not be surveyed, nor must it follow property

Table 2.2 Maximum Extraterritorial Jurisdiction for Cities

City Population	Maximum Extraterritorial Area
Up to 10,000	1 mile
10,000 to 25,000	2 miles
Over 25,000	3 miles

Figure 2.2 City Establishment of ETJ

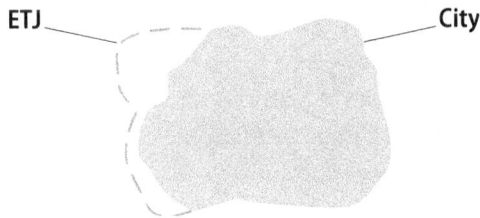

ETJ _____ City

A city can extend its ETJ to part of the area around the city without extending it to the entire potential ETJ area.

Figure 2.3 Overlapping ETJs

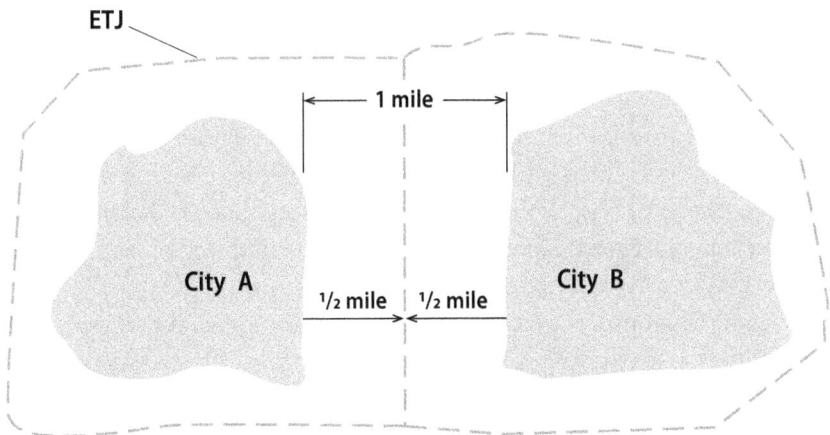

ETJ

1 mile

City A   ½ mile | ½ mile   City B

Where two cities' potential ETJ boundaries overlap, the ETJ boundary of each is set at the midpoint between the two cities.

lines. However, the boundary must be defined clearly enough that people can easily tell whether or not their property is within the city's jurisdiction. A very general boundary description, such as "one mile in all directions from city hall," would not be legally sufficient; boundary lines drawn on county tax maps would be.

A city's extraterritorial area boundary does not automatically change when the city's corporate boundaries change through annexation. If, for example, a city has adopted a one-mile ETJ area and the city subsequently extends its corporate boundaries by annexing out three-fourths of a mile, the ETJ boundary stays in the same place and the city then has an ETJ area of only one-quarter mile. The city can later amend the ETJ boundary to add territory up to a mile from the new city limit, but it must go through all of the proper steps of amending its ETJ boundary ordinance to do so.

In order to exercise extraterritorial jurisdiction, a city must adopt an extraterritorial boundary map ordinance. Once a city determines its proposed new ETJ boundary and formulates its extraterritorial boundary map ordinance, the city must set a date for a public hearing on the proposal and provide notice of the hearing to affected citizens. Notice of the hearing must appear once a week for two successive weeks, with the first notice appearing at least ten but not more than twenty-five days before the hearing. The city must also mail a notice of the hearing on the ETJ boundary ordinance to all affected property owners. This notice must explain the effects of the extension of jurisdiction and also advise these persons of the right to have extraterritorial representation on the city planning board and board of adjustment. The notice must be mailed at least four weeks prior to the hearing. Another mailed notice must be provided when the city extends its zoning ordinance to the area. The individual notice on the rezoning must be mailed at least ten days but no more than twenty-five days prior to the hearing (which is less than the four-week minimum required for the boundary ordinance mailing), so two mailings are necessary. If a city holds a single hearing on the ETJ ordinance and the application of the city's zoning ordinance, it must send two notices for the same hearing.

In some situations, the city must receive county approval to establish or extend its extraterritorial jurisdiction. Within the first mile, county approval is required only if the county is already exercising all three land use tools—county zoning, subdivision control, and building code enforcement—for that specific geographic area. County adoption of specialized ordinances, such as a water supply watershed protection ordinance or stormwater management ordinance, does not trigger the requirement for county approval of municipal extraterritorial jurisdiction. For extraterritorial jurisdictions extending more than one mile from the city, county approval is always required.

The county gives approval in a written resolution adopted by its county board of commissioners. There are no standards set for the county board to use in making the decision on whether to allow the city to have extraterritorial jurisdiction. That choice is left to the good judgment and discretion of the county commissioners. Several counties have adopted specific policy guidelines for their decisions on ETJ extension requests, such as requiring the city to show it has the capacity to apply and administer regulations in the area or that the area will be provided city utility services within a specified time. The county commissioners may rescind their written approval, but they must give the city two years' written notice before doing so (if the city and county are both agreed, the change can take place immediately).

Once the city council has followed these steps, it may adopt the extraterritorial boundary map ordinance by a simple majority vote. The city zoning of the area is also adopted by majority vote as the protest petition option is not applicable to a city's initial zoning of property added to its territory by annexation or ETJ expansion.

After adoption, the city must file a copy of the adopted map of the boundary of the ETJ area with the city clerk and with the county register of deeds. This is the official copy of the new boundary that citizens can check to determine whether or not their land is covered by city zoning regulations.

The city must also promptly move forward with an amendment to the maps in its zoning ordinance to apply zoning to this new territory, if that was not done when the ETJ boundary map was adopted. Just as when it annexes territory, when the city extends its ETJ into an area previously zoned by the county, the county zoning stays in effect for sixty days or until the city zoning takes effect, whichever occurs first.

Finally, after a city establishes extraterritorial jurisdiction, it must provide for representation by residents of this area on certain city boards. Residents of the extraterritorial area do not get to vote in city elections and do not pay city taxes. However, the city planning board and board of adjustment must be expanded to include residents of this area (or other county residents if there are not enough residents in the extraterritorial area itself). The statutes require a proportional number of extraterritorial members. That is, if a city

Figure 2.4 Summary of Procedural Requirements for Extraterritorial Land Use Planning and Regulation

Steps for Applying Extraterritorial Jurisdiction

1. *Prepare an adequate boundary description.* There is no requirement to have a surveyed line, but the boundary must be precise enough that landowners can determine without hiring a surveyor if they are included. Tax maps may be used as a base for drawing the lines.

2. *Publish the newspaper notice of a public hearing,* which must appear once a week for two successive weeks, with the first notice at least ten but not more than twenty-five days before the hearing.

3. *Mail notice to individual property owners in the affected area.* Mailed notice is required for the hearing on adoption of the extraterritorial boundary map itself. This notice must be sent four weeks prior to the hearing. A second mailing on the application of zoning is also required, and it must be mailed in the ten- to twenty-five-day period prior to the hearing.

4. *Secure county agreement if the county is exercising zoning power, regulating subdivisions, and enforcing the building code in the area affected or if the area extends more than one mile from the city.* A written, formal county resolution is required in either instance.

5. *Adopt ordinance by city governing board setting extraterritorial planning jurisdiction and its boundary.*

6. *File a copy of the boundary map with the city clerk and register of deeds.*

7. *Amend the city zoning ordinance to add the area to zoning maps.* Also, other city land use regulations—subdivision ordinances, building codes, housing codes, and so forth—being applied in the extraterritorial areas should be amended as well to specify whether they apply in the ETJ.

8. *Appoint extraterritorial members to the planning board and the board of adjustment.* Appointments are made by the county board of commissioners after a hearing on the appointments. The number of "outside" members relative to the number of "inside" members must be proportional to the population of the ETJ area relative to the city population. City appointments are allowed if the county fails to act.

---

has a population of 5,000 and it has a five-member board of adjustment, that means there is one board member for each 1,000 city residents. The city must therefore provide for one ETJ board member for each 1,000 ETJ residents. The county board of commissioners appoints county citizens to these city boards; if the county commissioners fail to make these appointments, the city council makes them.

Figure 2.4 provides an overview of the steps a city must take in order to establish or change its ETJ boundary.

Individual Local Agreements

Special legislation or local agreements allow exceptions to rules on geographic jurisdiction for zoning.

Cities commonly ask the North Carolina General Assembly for approval to extend their extraterritorial jurisdictions beyond the limits described above. A fast-growing city with a population under 10,000 may ask for the authority to have up to two miles of extraterritorial area. The legislature also can adopt special legislation setting respective extraterritorial boundaries in high-growth areas with multiple cities, as was done in Mecklenburg County. In some instances the legislature has removed authority to adopt ETJ for specific cities (in 2013 Asheville lost its ETJ authority).

Local agreements between a city and county may also create variations to the general jurisdictional rules. For example, a city can ask the county to apply county development regulations within the city. Two nearby cities can agree to an extraterritorial boundary that is not midway between their cities. Such local agreements must be in writing, be adopted by the governing boards of both governments involved, and be consistent with the rules described in this chapter. For example, a county cannot agree to let a city with a population under 10,000 extend its extraterritorial jurisdiction more than a mile; only the General Assembly can amend that standard.

Note

1. Report of the Municipal Government Study Commission of the North Carolina General Assembly 18 (Nov. 1958).

Chapter 3

Planning

A small town is presented with a proposal to rezone a large tract on the fringe of town to allow a new shopping center to be built. Would this be good for the town? A room full of neighbors opposes the issuance of a special use permit for an apartment building, contending it would snarl traffic, lead to overcrowded schools, and that the building would be incompatible with the character of their neighborhood. Would it? The utilities department has proposed that the county incur a substantial expense to extend a large water line well into a rural township in order to serve a potential new manufacturing plant (with a rezoning for the plant to be submitted in a few months). Would this be a good investment for the county?

While rezoning petitions and applications for permits often raise these questions, the development regulations themselves usually give little guidance on the underlying community policies that point the way to the "right" answers. That is where planning comes in. Planning is a tool local governments can employ to gather needed information, conduct detailed analysis, secure public participation, and undertake the careful deliberation that provide the context for and guide regulatory and public investment decisions.

Most local governments that have a zoning ordinance also have a comprehensive plan or a land use plan. The relationship between the plan and the zoning ordinance can be a powerful factor in land use regulation. But the plan is not a regulation, and in some communities little use is made of it. The strength of the relationship between plans and regulations in North Carolina is largely up to each local government, though the plan is growing in legal significance.

State Mandates

Many states require local governments to prepare land use plans. In those states there are usually requirements as to what the plan must include, how it is to be prepared, and the relationship of the plan to regulation. While the details vary significantly from state to state, in the Southeast alone Florida, Georgia, Tennessee, South Carolina, and Virginia all have statewide planning mandates. North Carolina has not joined this trend. Though several study commissions have examined the issue, there are few legal mandates regarding land use planning in this state.

The only mandate for local land use plans in North Carolina is the requirement of the Coastal Area Management Act, which requires that plans be prepared in the twenty coastal counties (municipalities in the coastal area can elect to prepare their own plans or be covered by a county plan). Yet even in the coastal area there is no requirement that there be zoning or other plan implementation and only a very limited requirement for consistency between the plans and any zoning that is enacted.

Recent legislation has, however, increased the role of planning in North Carolina. When acting on any proposed zoning amendment, local governments must carefully consider their adopted plans and note in a written statement whether the amendment is consistent with those plans. Local governments are eligible for state disaster assistance only if they have an approved hazard mitigation plan. Adoption of a plan is also a factor in local government priority for a variety of state environmental and infrastructure funding. Cities are required to develop transportation plans, and the state Department of Transportation can participate only if the affected jurisdictions have adopted a land development plan within the previous five years. (Counties have the option of doing likewise.)

The Comprehensive Plan

Despite the fact that land use plans are not required outside the coastal area, a fairly consistent pattern of local comprehensive planning has emerged in North Carolina. Many cities and counties have undertaken planning efforts to help guide the future of their communities.

The comprehensive plan is traditionally used by local governments as their principal planning tool. This plan takes a long-range perspective—

typically ten to twenty years—and looks at the interrelationships between land uses, transportation, utilities, recreation, neighborhood revitalization, historic preservation, and the like. It is common for these plans to focus on physical development.

The planning effort usually involves substantial data collection and technical analysis, public discussion of a vision for the community, and attempts to reach consensus on what the community should be like in the future and how that will be achieved. The planning process involves examination of changes in population and development and consideration of the need for and ability to provide necessary public services like water, sewer, schools, parks, roads, police, fire, and emergency services. It also involves consideration of the preservation and enhancement of important community attributes such as a clean and healthy environment, good quality jobs and housing, vibrant commercial areas, historic structures and community aesthetics, and other important concerns.

Good planning is a cooperative venture involving professional staff or consultants, citizen advisory boards, affected citizens and interest groups, and elected officials. The planning board usually serves a key organizational role. The planning board often provides guidance to the staff, coordinates public participation, debates the overall public interest, and makes recommendations for action to the governing board. Preparing or updating a plan usually takes six to eighteen months, depending on the complexity of the issues to be addressed and the amount of change since the last plan update. A typical plan update schedule is about every five years.

In addition to the comprehensive plan, many cities and counties undertake a variety of other planning efforts that can guide zoning decisions. A small area or neighborhood plan can provide greater detail or focus to the more general plan. A strategic plan may be developed to prepare a communitywide action plan to address several high-priority issues. Plans are often also prepared for various specific government functions, such as a transportation plan, recreation plan, housing plan, downtown revitalization plan, or stormwater control plan. Many local governments also have specialized plans, such as design guidelines that may address architectural standards in commercial areas or historic districts, landscaping guidelines, or plans for the appearance of major transportation corridors. Any plan that has been officially adopted by the city or county must be considered in zoning decisions.

The purpose of these planning efforts is the establishment of clear, consistent, predictable, coordinated community policies that will serve as the long-term foundation for day-to-day public investment and regulatory decisions.

Ordinance Consistency with Adopted Plans

Plans are *not* regulations. They do not have binding legal effect; they are advisory only. Development regulations (such as zoning or subdivision regulations) and capital improvement programs are necessary for plan implementation. If a community does adopt a land use plan, there is no legal requirement that all zoning decisions exactly match up to it. The plan is just that—a plan or guide and not a regulation. But the plan, and all of the studies and discussion that led to it, does provide the general policy foundation for regulatory decisions. The law, as well as good planning practice and common sense, suggests that those policies be carefully considered as each zoning decision is made.

State zoning statutes provide that all zoning must be "in accordance with a comprehensive plan." The North Carolina courts have not, however, read this to mean that all zoning decisions must be precisely measured against a separately adopted land use plan. Rather, the courts have ruled that zoning decisions must be based on a reasoned consideration of land use issues facing the entire community, which means that competent technical studies must serve as the foundation of zoning decisions and that such studies and plans and public input must be thoroughly considered as zoning decisions are made. A zoning amendment that is clearly contrary to the policies in an adopted city or county plan, particularly if the rezoning involves only a small area of land, is suspect and may well be invalidated by the courts unless a clear public purpose for the amendment has been established. (See the discussion of spot zoning in Chapter 9.)

Furthermore, cities and counties must explicitly consider their adopted plans when acting on proposed amendments to a zoning ordinance. The planning board is required to make a written report on plan consistency to the city council or county board of commissioners as part of the amendment review process. The governing board must then approve a written statement that addresses plan consistency when it approves or rejects any proposed zoning text or map amendment. The board's statement must describe how the action is or is not consistent with the plan and briefly explain why the board considers the action reasonable and in the public interest.

A city council or board of county commissioners may adopt a zoning amendment that is inconsistent with adopted plans so long as the council or board acknowledges in writing that it knows it is doing so and sets out the rationale for its decision. The statutes do not require detailed findings, just the brief statement as described.

While a local government has the legal authority to act inconsistently with its plan, whether and when it should do so are more complicated questions and present a policy choice for the board. A prudent governing board carefully considers the comprehensive plan. If the board intends to act contrary to plan policies, it must explain why. After all, presumptively the plan was based on solid technical analysis and broad public participation and has been used by landowners, investors, and residents as a guide for future land uses. The policies in the plan often create a set of expectations that many citizens may be relying upon. But the plan does not set policies in stone. Situations evolve and facts change, as do the policy choices of elected officials. These officials are free to make the decisions they believe will best serve their citizens (and the citizens can address the wisdom of those choices at the next election). The plan assists officials in making more deliberate, thoughtful decisions. The statutes mandate that it be considered. But ultimately decisions about zoning and other land use regulations are left to the good judgment of elected local government officials.

Chapter 4

Zoning Ordinances

Zoning ordinances are the basic land use regulation most commonly used in North Carolina and around the country. Zoning ordinances may be adopted as separate ordinances or incorporated as a section of an overall unified development ordinance that also includes subdivision and other development regulations.

History
The Origins of Zoning

Prior to the 1920s, landowners generally relied on nuisance suits to protect their rights if one neighbor used his or her land in a manner that harmed others, and some local governments had construction codes and regulations addressing individual noxious land uses. But with increasing urbanization, the need to know the rules of the development game in advance and the inefficiency of individual private law suits to protect neighborhoods and communities, zoning regulations emerged as the preferred means of addressing these concerns.

The precursors to zoning ordinances were regulations on particular uses. In the late 1800s and early 1900s, local governments in the United States began to enact ordinances to regulate where certain kinds of businesses could locate and how big certain kinds of buildings could be. Early examples include an 1885 Modesto, California, ordinance regulating the location of laundries; ordinances regulating building heights in Washington, D.C., in 1899 and in Boston in 1904; and a 1909 Los Angeles ordinance restricting the siting of industrial plants. The Modesto ordinance is notable not only because it is among the earliest examples of a city regulating the location of particular types of businesses, but also because it shows just how controversial such regulations can be. For years people have argued whether the Modesto ordinance had the noble purpose of minimizing the harmful impacts of commercial laundries on adjacent residential areas or the ignoble purpose of racial discrimination against the Chinese immigrants who were the proprietors of most of the regulated laundries.

In 1916 New York City developed the nation's first comprehensive zoning ordinance. The construction of a subway system and the development of high-rise construction had created a hazardous situation. Buildings were so close together and contained so many people that inadequate ventilation and fire safety were serious problems. In addition, the increasingly crowded city was facing complaints generated when businesses, industries, and residential areas were located too close to one another. Separation of the social classes also played a role in motivating the move to adopt zoning in New York. Proprietors of exclusive shops along Fifth Avenue complained that low-income workers from nearby garment factories were crowding the sidewalks and driving away prosperous customers, prompting the shopkeepers to call for zoning restrictions to move the factories to a more distant location. To address all these issues, the city adopted a comprehensive zoning ordinance.

The problems with incompatible land uses, traffic, noise, congestion, and loss of amenities were certainly not confined to New York City. Neither was the desire to keep certain types of industry, business, and housing (and perhaps the people who lived and worked in them) in their "proper" place. As the nation shifted from a rural to an urban population, people were increasingly affected by neighbors' land uses. In 1800, less than 4 percent of the nation's population lived in cities. By 1920 that figure had passed 50 percent, and the national drive to develop new ways to deal with land use management took off.

Cities around the country soon adopted the New York zoning model. The U.S. Department of Commerce promoted the zoning concept by encouraging all the states to grant to their local governments the power to adopt zoning ordinances. After circulating drafts for several years, in 1922 the Department of Commerce, under the leadership of then-Secretary Herbert Hoover, published a model state zoning-enabling code. The national movement to adopt zoning ordinances got a big boost in 1926 when the United States Supreme Court ruled the zoning concept constitutional.[1]

In the period after World War I, the national trend to adopt zoning took hold in North Carolina. Many cities had by then already adopted some rudimentary land use regulations, but most regulations addressed only such issues as the location of individual buildings considered nuisances or fire hazards, such as wooden buildings in the center of cities. In 1923 the General Assembly adopted the model legislation proposed by the Department of Commerce and gave cities the authority to adopt zoning ordinances. By the late 1920s a dozen of the larger cities in the state had zoning ordinances.

The state's rapid population growth after World War II fueled the public demand for land use management in places well beyond the state's largest cities. By the 1960s most of North Carolina's cities and towns had adopted zoning ordinances. Zoning came later to rural areas. While a few of the most urbanized counties had local legislation authorizing zoning, counties were not granted general zoning authority until 1959, and it was not until the 1980s and 1990s that many counties adopted zoning.

The Evolution of Zoning

Zoning is now widely used in North Carolina and around the nation. Currently more than 550 cities and 80 counties in North Carolina have adopted zoning ordinances.[2] Almost all of the state's cities with populations over 1,000 have a zoning ordinance. Over 90 percent of the state's population resides in areas subject to zoning. Figure 2.1 on page 16 illustrates which counties have full, partial, or no zoning (see Chapter 2 for more details on city and county zoning jurisdiction). Yet there remains great interest in protecting private property rights and great skepticism about governmental regulatory programs. What explains the endurance—and even expansion—of zoning?

For one thing, zoning has become our principal tool for protecting property values and providing a stable real estate market. By using zoning to prevent incompatible uses from being too close together and by providing a degree of predictability about future land uses, local governments provide a degree of stability to the land market that property owners and developers both find reassuring. Other mechanisms, such as developers instituting private restrictive covenants and citizens filing nuisance suits against their neighbors, are far less predictable and effective means of accomplishing such goals. Zoning is valuable in other respects as well. It can help foster economic development, protect aesthetic and environmental resources, facilitate the more efficient provision of public services, and protect and enhance the character of a given community.

Over the years, North Carolina's enabling legislation for zoning has evolved in several ways, becoming broader in some areas and more specific in others. The state has provided local governments with the authority to use more regulatory tools for land use management. For example, local governments can now use conditional zoning to tailor regulations to individual projects and can regulate and protect historic structures and neighborhoods. The state (and, increasingly, the federal government) mandates protection for a few kinds of facilities (such as manufactured homes, family-care homes, and telecommunication towers) to keep local land use regulations from unduly restricting them. These limits are discussed in more detail in Chapter 14. The state has imposed rigorous procedural requirements on local land use regulation, such as mailed notice requirements for hearings on proposed rezonings and quasi-judicial permit applications. The state has mandated that local land use regulations protect natural resources of critical importance, such as water supply watersheds and mountain ridges. Federal mandates on stormwater management require local land use regulations. Finally, the state has mandated that proposed developments receiving local approvals be protected from some subsequent changes in zoning regulations. In addition, cities or counties can and often do secure legislative approval of modest individual variations in the zoning power for their own local governments only.

Just as state legislation on zoning has evolved in character and complexity over the past seventy-five years, so have local zoning ordinances. As recently as 1958, the entire zoning code for the City of Charlotte was less than twenty pages long. Now a zoning ordinance for a small town is rarely less than a hundred pages long and the zoning ordinances for larger jurisdictions are typically well over five hundred pages long. What happened?

The first major change was an increase in the number of zoning districts. Many early zoning ordinances had only three districts—one each for residential, commercial, and industrial uses. Contemporary zoning ordinances frequently have twenty or thirty districts. For example, rather than a single commercial district, there may be different districts for downtown commercial, shopping centers, highway commercial, and neighborhood commercial. A second change has been to include standards on a broader range of topics, such as off-street parking, signs, storm-water control, historic preservation, manufactured home parks, and landscaping. Zoning districts and standards are discussed in more detail below. A third change has been to add more flexibility to the ordinances through inclusion of special and conditional use permits. These are discussed in more detail in Chapter 10. Ordinances have been expanded to include standards and procedures for making these decisions. All of these factors have added to the length and complexity of zoning ordinances.

It is also increasingly common for cities and counties to merge the zoning, subdivision, and all other development-related ordinances into a single ordinance—generally referred to as a unified development ordinance and often called the UDO. This allows coordination and consolidation of ordinance provisions but leads to an even larger ordinance.

Content of Ordinances
Use Districts and the Zoning Map

A zoning ordinance can be an imposing document. Zoning ordinances often include several hundred pages of mind-numbing detail. To further complicate matters, each ordinance is unique—there is no standardized format, content, or even terminology for zoning ordinances. For example, a zoning district named "R-10" in one ordinance may allow single-family homes on 10,000-square-foot lots, but in another zoning ordinance an R-10 district may allow multifamily residential units at a density of ten units per acre. Differences between one ordinance and the next, however, allow cities and counties to tailor specific provisions to address local needs and government policies. Despite the lack of uniformity, ordinances do typically address certain issues and contain some common features—elements found in most zoning ordinances.

While most city and county ordinances—from taxes to dog licensing—apply uniformly throughout the jurisdiction, zoning sets different standards for different parts of a jurisdiction. To accomplish this, a zoning ordinance must contain a map as well as detailed textual instructions. First, the text of the ordinance describes what land uses are permitted in each district, what development standards have to be met in that district, and the like (see Figure 4.1). Second, a map places the land in the jurisdiction into various zoning districts (see Figure 4.2). Use of these zones is why the ordinance is called "zoning." This map is an official part of the zoning ordinance. Any

Can a City Really Do Zoning? The *Aydlett* Case

In the earliest days of zoning, it was unclear whether the courts would uphold use of zoning and, if so, what legal constraints the courts would impose. In 1931 the North Carolina Supreme Court resolved many of these questions in an early landmark decision on zoning. This colorful case involved feuding neighbors, a stubborn landowner, and an unyielding city government, all engaged in a five-year-long battle over the use of a single lot in Elizabeth City. This fight produced four state supreme court decisions and was ultimately resolved by a special act of the legislature.

The land involved in this case was a fashionable residential block adjacent to the downtown area of Elizabeth City, then a town of about 10,000 people. Mr. A. L. "Ab" Aydlett resided on the corner of this block nearest downtown. Aydlett's brother, Mr. E. F. Aydlett, a prominent local attorney and perhaps the most influential political figure in the region, owned the Southern Hotel, located on the edge of the downtown business area just across the street from Ab Aylett's corner lot. In the spring of 1928, E. F. Aydlett spent some $100,000 (a considerable sum at that time) to renovate the hotel so it could compete with a new rival hotel in town. (See the illustration on page 37 for a contemporary postcard view of the Southern Hotel.) Ab Aydlett then proposed to put a new gas station on his corner residential lot. The neighbors strenuously objected to the proposed gas station and convinced the city council in July 1928 to adopt an ordinance prohibiting gas stations in this residential block.

In 1931, in *Elizabeth City v. Aydlett*, the court upheld a zoning ordinance prohibition against future filling stations in residential districts, but existing stations were allowed to remain. Two years later, however, the owner of this site got local legislation passed to allow construction of the station, which was later reconstructed and operated for many years (Courtesy Museum of the Albemarle, Elizabeth City, N.C.).

This was far from the end of the matter. In February 1929 Aydlett erected a wooden shack on his lot, right next to the street and his neighbor's property. His next-door neighbor complained to the local paper that Aydlett was just trying to block his views and make the neighbors' property as undesirable as possible in retaliation for their stopping his gas station project. In April the city council, by a four-to-three vote, refused to amend the gas station ordinance to allow construction of a station on this lot. Undeterred, in August Aydlett demolished part of his residence, moved the rest to the side of the lot, and began construction of his gas station on the corner without the city's approval. The station is pictured on page 36. The opinions quoted on the front page of the August 2, 1929, edition of a local paper, *The Independent*, could have been from people in many contemporary zoning disputes. "It's my property, I'll do with it what I please," said Aydlett. The city's response: "The thrift and enterprise of all the people of the city have contributed to the upbuilding of your property and you have no right to devote your property to a purpose that would be destructive of the property values of other residents." Both sides agreed the matter would soon head to court, although it is doubtful they knew how long their case would stay entangled there.

The city promptly issued Aydlett a criminal citation for violation of the gas station ordinance. On September 10, 1929, Aydlett won his first legal battle when the trial court declared the gas station ordinance unconstitutional because it did not apply citywide and because it exempted existing gas stations. The fact that Ab was represented by his brother, E. F., and that the trial court judge was E. F.'s son-in-law, no doubt aided his case. The city appealed the decision and got an injunction to prohibit work on the station while the case was on appeal.

continued

Postcard view of Southern Hotel (Courtesy Willard E. Jones Collection, Ahoskie, N.C.)

At the same time the city headed on another tack. In August 1929 the city resurrected its moribund planning commission and asked it to develop a zoning ordinance. The planning commission examined newly adopted zoning ordinances in Raleigh, Durham, High Point, Rocky Mount, Richmond, and Norfolk. In early September the commission proposed a zoning ordinance for Elizabeth City. On October 1 the city held a public hearing on the proposed zoning ordinance, and not a single person appeared to oppose it. The big news of the day was not the zoning hearing, but the announcement that the region's first talking picture equipment was to be installed in the city's Carolina Theater later in October. On October 7, 1929, the city adopted its first comprehensive zoning ordinance. The ordinance put Aydlett's lot in a business zoning district, but one that did not allow gas stations. So the great gas station battle continued.

On April 9, 1930, the North Carolina Supreme Court ruled that the city should not have been granted an injunction to enforce the gas station ordinance after Aydlett had been acquitted on the criminal charge. So Aydlett began work the next Monday to finish building his gas station. But the city was in court by Monday evening to get the work stopped. By Wednesday the station was half built but the court ordered work halted. Both sides again appealed, with the mayor telling the local paper, "We'll fight this thing to the last ditch."

The parties were back in court in May 1930. This time Aydlett had hired plumbers to install water lines to his station and they had tunneled under the city sidewalk to do so, prompting yet another city suit. The parties were back before the same judge, the son-in-law of Ab's brother and attorney. The city attorney and judge promptly got into a heated dispute that nearly landed the city's lawyer in jail. The judge opined, "The City doesn't give a rap whether or not Mr. Aydlett tunnels under a sidewalk. I see this case as nothing at all but spite work on the part of the City. I shall not prosecute any such case in my court. The City ordinance may be valid, but I'm going to dismiss the case. I have no patience with the small methods and tactics of the City in fighting Mr. Aydlett." When the city attorney responded that he took this to mean he should not bring any more indictments for violations of the law, the judge threatened him with jail for contempt of court. The incident led to a spirited but unsuccessful effort to unseat the judge in the June 1930 elections. It did not, however, deter either side from continued legal battles. For example, when Aydlett asked for city approval to remove the curbs to install a driveway into the station, the city denied approval. Aydlett tore up the curbs anyway, and the city took him to court in 1930 for that as well. In any event, the structure was completed in 1930, but it sat vacant for another three years while the legal battles continued.

When the second round of cases made it to the state supreme court in 1931, the issue was compliance with the zoning ordinance. The court issued three opinions in this last stage of the case. In the first, it concluded that injunctions could be used to enforce zoning. In the second, the court said injunctions could be used to prevent interference with city sidewalks, trees, and streetlights. In the third and most important of these cases, the 1931 landmark opinion *Elizabeth City v. Aydlett*[a] the court upheld the constitutionality of zoning in North Carolina. The court also ruled that a land use (in this instance, gas stations) could be completely prohibited from a particular zoning district

This structure was eventually built on the Aydlett site (note the Southern Hotel in the background).

and that new uses could be prohibited without requiring similar existing uses to be closed. Both of these points were essential to the legal and political viability of zoning, and the case cleared the way for widespread adoption of zoning by North Carolina cities.

Even though the city won an important legal battle with this landmark court case, it still eventually lost the Great Gas Station War. Having lost with the city council and in the courts, Aydlett was more successful with the state legislature. In the spring of 1931, before the supreme court's ruling upholding zoning, the General Assembly had almost short-circuited the whole matter. A local bill to exempt the gas station from the city's zoning passed the House of Representatives but was killed in a Senate committee. (A local supporter of the bill claimed it lost only because Ab's station was leased to Gulf and one of the Senate committee members had a cousin who worked for Texaco.) In 1933 the matter got to the General Assembly a second time. This time the legislature adopted a local bill allowing gasoline service stations in any Elizabeth City zoning district that allowed "retail stores, shoe shops, barber shops, pressing shops, restaurants, confectioneries, offices, hotels, theaters, assembly halls, newsstands, wholesaling or jobbing"—which, not coincidentally, just happened to describe the uses allowed in the district that covered Aydlett's lot. Aydlett was finally able to legally open his gas station.

The gas station operated on this corner in downtown Elizabeth City for some thirty years. The original gas station was soon replaced with a more substantial building occupying the entire corner lot. That structure, shown in the photo above, served as a gas station for many years and was eventually converted to other business uses, ranging from TV sales to a health food store. Eighty-five years later, the building is still being put to commercial use in its present incarnation as a coffee shop.

---

a. 201 N.C. 602 (1931).

change in the map to move land from one zoning district to another, a process called a rezoning, is an amendment of the ordinance and must follow all of the procedures required for zoning amendments.

Early zoning ordinances provided only a few broad zoning districts. Land was generally placed in one of three districts: a residential district, a business district, or an industrial district. These early ordinances also typically set these districts up as *cumulative* districts. That is, the residential district would be the most restrictive and no other land uses would be allowed in it. The business districts would allow both businesses and residential uses. The industrial districts were the least restrictive, allowing industrial, business, and residential uses. Figure 4.3 illustrates the "zoning pyramid" that was established by these cumulative zoning districts. The primary objectives of these early ordinances were separation of incompatible land uses and the protection of residential property values, both of which could be accomplished with this basic approach.

This early arrangement of use districts has become substantially more complicated. A contemporary zoning ordinance usually contains a number of conventional, overlay, floating, and conditional districts.

Conventional zoning districts allow a variety of permitted uses. Over time the range of uses allowed in a single district has become progressively narrower. As local governments have more finely tuned and limited the permitted uses in each district, the number of different zoning districts has multiplied. For example, instead of a single residential district, a modern zoning ordinance may have five or ten different residential districts—one for single-family residences on large lots, one for single-family residences on small lots, one for multifamily residences, and another for mobile homes. Similarly, a single business district may now be subdivided into separate zoning districts for neighborhood business, highway commercial, central business, and shopping center uses. While a small town or rural county ordinance may still only have five to ten zoning districts, a typical contemporary city zoning ordinance may now have twenty or thirty different zoning districts. A recent trend in zoning has been to reexamine this proliferation of districts and consider allowing a greater range of uses within individual districts. The number of districts and what range of uses is allowed in each are key policy choices for local governments amending and modernizing their ordinances. Most North Carolina zoning ordinances have a dozen or so conventional zoning districts.[3]

Figure 4.1 Sample Zoning Ordinance Text

CHAPTER 4

ZONING

DISTRICTS AND USES

9-4-1 DISTRICTS ESTABLISHED

All property within the jurisdiction shall be divided into zoning districts with designations and purposes listed in Section 9-4-2 (District Descriptions).

9-4-2 DISTRICT DESCRIPTIONS

(a) General Use Districts

(1) Agricultural:

AG AGRICULTURAL DISTRICT

The AG, Agricultural District is primarily intended to accommodate uses of an agricultural nature including farm residences and farm tenant housing. It also accommodates scattered nonfarm residences on large tracts of land. It is not intended for major residential subdivisions. The district is established for the following purposes:

a. to preserve the use of land for agricultural, forest, and open space purposes until urban development is enabled by the extension of essential urban services;

b. to provide for the orderly transition to urban uses by preventing premature conversion of farmland;

c. to discourage any use that would create premature or extraordinary public infrastructure and service demands; or

d. to discourage scattered commercial and industrial land uses.

(2) Single-Family Residential:

In the following districts the number refers to the minimum lot size in thousands of square feet.

a. RS-40 RESIDENTIAL SINGLE FAMILY DISTRICT

The RS-40, Residential Single Family District is primarily intended to accommodate single family detached dwellings on large lots in areas without access to public water and sewer services. The district is established to promote single family detached residences where environmental features (such as within water

4-1

The text of a zoning ordinance defines the use districts, development standards, and procedures to be used in zoning.

Figure 4.2 Zoning Districts

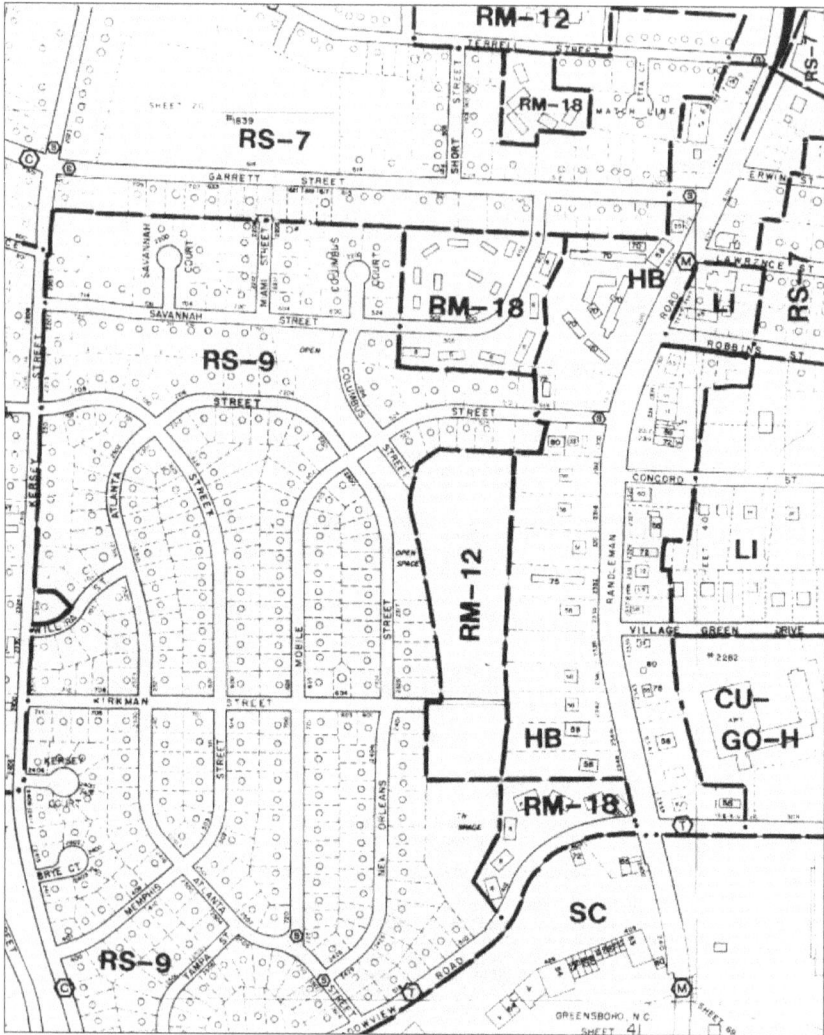

Each zoning ordinance includes a map that places the land subject to zoning in various zoning districts.

Zoning districts now are rarely cumulative. While many zoning ordinances were originally adopted primarily to protect residential property values, modern zoning addresses broader public purposes, such as promoting economic development. A local government may determine that because of utility, highway, and rail access, an area should be reserved exclusively for

Figure 4.3 Hierarchy of Uses in Early Zoning Districts

Type of District	Uses Allowed		
	Residential Use	Business Use	Industrial Use
Residential	•		
Business	•	•	
Industrial	•	•	•

future industrial development. If an area particularly suited for industrial development were to be developed for residential use, industrial development would have to be located elsewhere, and local government might have to provide new services at considerable expense—if in fact any other suitable sites even existed. Also, if part of the area were first developed for residential uses, its residents might want to keep future industry out of their residential neighborhood. To prevent these difficulties and keep the site available for future industrial or commercial uses, many cities now no longer permit residential uses in these zoning districts.

Overlay zones are now a common feature of zoning ordinances. These are special zones in which requirements are imposed in addition to the basic or underlying zoning district requirements. For example, if a river runs through a city, special flood hazard requirements (such as special setback, building elevation, or flood-proofing requirements) may be imposed on all property lying within the flood hazard area adjacent to the river. So a new "floodplain" overlay zoning district is created that contains all of the special flood hazard development standards, and that district is applied to all land in the flood hazard area. But the new district does not replace whatever zoning district was already in place; rather, it acts in addition to—or overlays—the basic conventional use districts, whether they are residential, business, or industrial. Development in the overlay district must comply with requirements of both the overlay district and conventional district (see Figure 4.4). Typical overlay districts include floodplain districts, historic districts, airport districts, and highway corridor districts. It is less common but also possible to have an overlay district that relaxes the standards for particular uses.

Floating zones are specialized districts used in many ordinances. These zoning districts are defined and set out in the text of the ordinance but not applied on the ground unless and until a landowner petitions to rezone his or her property to one of these districts. For example, a mobile home park

Figure 4.4   Overlay District Requirements

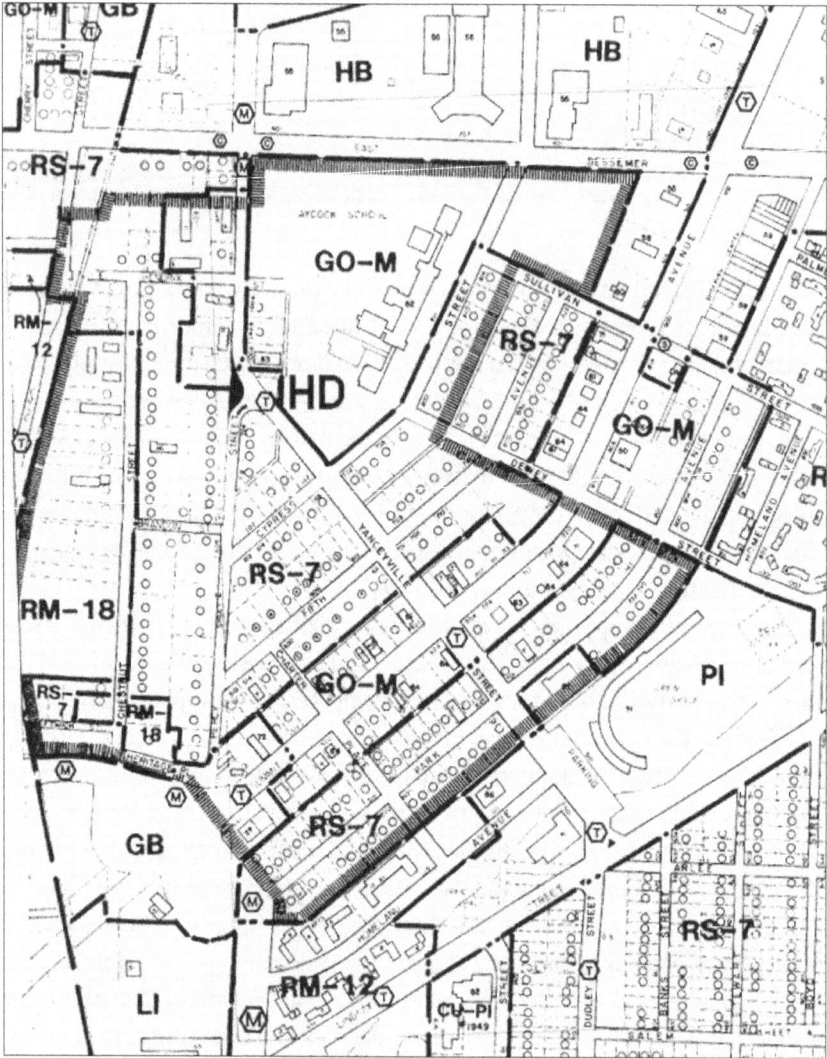

When an overlay district is adopted, the requirements of both the underlying zoning district and the special overlay district apply. In the example pictured above, the land within the bold, cross-hatched line must comply with the zoning ordinance's overlay historic district standards (thus the "HD") as well as meet the standards for whatever basic zoning district it is in (such as the RM-18, RS-7, or GO-M district).

district may be included in the zoning text to define the development standards for these uses—the densities allowed, road standards, minimum total size, and so forth. But the district is not applied to the zoning map unless and until a landowner asks for it.

Modern zoning ordinances have been criticized for being too rigid in their separation of uses, for producing sterile neighborhoods with no commercial uses, and for unduly separating homes from workplaces and shopping. Ironically, one of the early responses to this criticism was creation of yet another zoning district, a floating zone called a planned unit development (PUD) district. These districts allow a large site to be developed with a mixture of land uses according to an approved overall site plan. For example, a large tract may be developed with a mix of single-family and multifamily housing, with part of the site also devoted to commercial and office uses. Other PUD districts allow greater flexibility in dimensional standards (such as lot sizes and setbacks) upon approval of an overall master plan for the entire development. It is important to remember that zoning an area does not require a rigid separation of different land uses even though that is the way many ordinances have been structured. Each city and county can custom design its ordinance to include whatever number and type of districts and use restrictions seem appropriate in that particular place.

Contemporary zoning ordinances increasingly address this concern by adding a "mixed use" overlay or conventional district to allow greater flexibility amongst the types of uses permitted or a "traditional neighborhood" district to reduce lot size or setback requirements. These districts are adopted to accommodate houses clustered on smaller lots, with some neighborhood-scale commercial and office development and a strong pedestrian focus. These are sometimes referred to as "traditional neighborhood districts," "pedestrian oriented development," or "transit oriented development" districts.

Zoning districts may also be created that include detailed site-specific conditions, a practice known as *conditional* zoning. A local government electing to use this type of district must exercise great care, as enforceable individual conditions cannot be included in conventional zoning districts. Chapter 9 addresses the special issues that must be considered for conditional zoning districts. In North Carolina these districts are floating zones that can be created only at the landowner's request.

Use Restrictions

Within each zoning district there is a list of permitted uses. These are sometimes called "uses by right" because they are automatically allowed in that district. For example, a zoning district might list single-family residences, fire and police stations, schools, places of worship, and temporary construction offices as permitted uses in a particular residential zoning district.

It is impossible to list every potential land use that might be proposed in the future. Thus, a zoning ordinance must be carefully crafted to handle uses that are not explicitly addressed in the ordinance. Many ordinances contain several broad categories of uses, such as "other commercial uses," and specify where they can be located. Others prohibit any use not listed as permitted. Still others direct that unlisted uses are treated the same as the most nearly similar listed use. The courts have said that any ambiguity in the ordinance as to whether a particular use is permitted should be resolved in favor of the landowner.

Some older zoning cases from other states have held that it would be inappropriate to totally exclude an otherwise lawful use from the entire jurisdiction. Some uses—manufactured housing, telecommunication towers, and adult entertainment are examples—are protected from total exclusion by statutory or constitutional provisions. These types of uses are discussed in Chapters 14 and 15. In North Carolina the courts generally defer to the legislative judgment of elected policy-making officials. The choice of whether and where to allow a particular use is presumed by the courts to be valid unless it is arbitrary and capricious. The courts have, for example, routinely upheld decisions by jurisdictions to completely ban off-premise commercial advertising signs. A governing body, however, should consider context—the type of use, its impacts, the size and character of the regulated area, and so forth—in zoning deliberations. If a small, largely residential town excludes a heavy industrial use because there is just no place in the jurisdiction it can be located without substantial harmful impacts on its neighbors, the decision to exclude such uses would not be an arbitrary policy choice. On the other hand, total exclusion of a particular industrial use by a large city with substantial industrial areas may indeed be considered arbitrary. Before a governing board adopts a ban on a use, the board should identify the negative impacts of the use, discuss alternative measures to prevent those impacts, and explore the impacts of excluding the use. Only then should a potential total ban be considered.

In recent decades most zoning ordinances have added provisions allowing some "maybes" between those uses that are automatically permitted and those that are prohibited in a particular district. The local government may determine that certain uses are suitable for a particular zoning district if (but only if) specified conditions are met and only after detailed individual review. For example, it may determine that a multifamily residential development is permissible in a single-family zoning district if the development will be on a site of at least 2 acres, there is a 20-foot-wide vegetated buffer maintained between the development and adjacent single-family lots, and the project is designed to be compatible with the surrounding neighborhood. Such uses are allowed only after an individual makes an application for the use and local government approves it and grants a permit for it.

A zoning ordinance calls these uses conditional uses or special uses (and some older ordinances call them special exceptions), terms that are interchangeable, having the same legal definition. The zoning ordinance itself must set out the standards (or conditions) under which each conditional use will be allowed. The city or county is prohibited from making an ad hoc, case-by-case discretionary review of each project; the ordinance itself must spell out the standards for obtaining such a permit and a specific list of allowable uses. When someone wants to apply for a conditional use permit, a town or county board holds a hearing to take evidence on whether the project meets these standards. The governing board, the planning board, or the board of adjustment is responsible for holding a hearing and making the decision. Staff members may not make decisions on special or conditional use permits. These types of permits are discussed in more detail in Chapter 10.

Many zoning ordinances contain a table or schedule of permitted uses that graphically displays how each use is treated in each district—which uses are permitted and which require a special or conditional use permit. Figure 4.5 illustrates a typical list of permitted uses.

Dimensional Requirements

In addition to specifying which kinds of land uses are permitted in each zoning district, zoning ordinances also have standards for what sizes of lots and buildings are allowed. Standards for lots typically specify minimum lot size and minimum construction setbacks. For example, a particular residential zoning district may require a minimum lot size of 10,000 square

Figure 4.5   Zoning Table of Uses

TABLE 30-4-5-1 PERMITTED USE SCHEDULE

ZONING DISTRICTS

USE TYPES	Ref SIC	AG	RS 4	RS 3	RS 2	RS 1	RS 1	RS 9	RS 7	RS 5	RM 5	RM 8	RM 1	RM 2	LO M	GO H	GO	N	LB	GB	HB	CB	SC	CP	LI	HI	PI	LC
RECREATIONAL USES (CONTINUED)																												
Public Parks	7990	D	D	D	D	D	D	D	D	D	D	D	D	D	D	D	D	D	D	D	D	D	D	D	D	D		1
Public Recreation Facilities	7990	D	D	D	D	D	D	D	D	D	D	D	D	D	D	D	D	D	D	D	D	D	D	D	D	D		2
Riding Stables	7999	S	S																								S	2
Shooting Ranges, Indoor	7999	S																	D	D					D	D		3
Shooting Ranges, Outdoor	7999	S																									S	5
Skating Rinks	7999																		P	P	P	P		P				3
Sports Instructional Schools	7999	S																P	P	P	P	D	P	P			P	3
Sports & Recreation Clubs, Indoor	7997																	P	P	P	P	P	P				P	3
Swim and Tennis Clubs	7997	S	S	S	S	S	S	S	S	S	S	S	S	S	D	D							D				D	3
EDUCATIONAL AND INSTITUTIONAL USES																												
Ambulance Services	4119	P													P	P		P	P	P	P	P	P	P	P	P	P	3
Auditoriums, Coliseums, or Stadiums	0000																	P	P	P	P		P				P	3
Cemeteries/Mausoleums	0000	D	D	D	D	D	D	D	D	D	D	D	D	D	D	D	D	D	D	D	D	D	D	D	D	D		2
Churches	8661	P	D	D	D	D	D	D	D	D	D	D	D	D	P	P	P	P	P	P	P	P	P	P	P	P	P	3
Colleges or Universities	8220															P		P									P	3
Correctional Institutions	9223	S																							S	S	S	4
Day Care Centers, Adult (5 or less, Hom. Occ)	8322	D	D	D	D	D	D	D	D	D	D	D	D	D	D	D	D	D	D	D	D	D	D	D	D	D	D	1
Day Care Centers, Adult (6 or More)	8322	S										D	D	D	D	D	D	D	D	D	D	D	D	D			D	3
Day Care Centers, Child (5 or less, Hom. Occ)	8351	D	D	D	D	D	D	D	D	D	D	D	D	D	D	D	D	D	D	D	D	D	D	D			D	1
Day Care Centers, Child (6 or more)	8351	S										D	D	D	D	D	D	D	D	D	D	D	D	D			D	3
Elementary or Secondary Schools	8211	D	D	D	D	D	D	D	D	D	D	D	D	D													P	3
Fire Stations	9224	P	P	P	P	P	P	P	P	P	P	P	P	P	P	P	P	P	P	P	P	P	P	P	P	P	P	3
Fraternities or Sororities (Univ. or College)	0000														D	D		D	D	D							P	3
Government Offices	9000														P	P	P	P	P	P	P	P	P	P	P	P	P	3
Hospitals	8062																										P	3
Libraries	8231														P	P	P	P	P	P	P	P	P	P			P	3
Museums or Art Galleries	8412														P	P	P	P	P	P	P	P	P	P			P	3
Nursing and Convalescent Homes	8050										S	S			P	P		P	P	P	P	P	P				P	3
Orphanages	8361	S									S	S			P	P		P	P								P	3
Police Stations, Neighborhood	9221	P	P	P	P	P	P	P	P	P	P	P	P	P	P	P	P	P	P	P	P	P	P	P	P	P	P	3
Post Offices	0000														P	P	P	P	P	P	P	P	P	P	P	P	P	3
Psychiatric Hospitals	8063														P	P			P	P							P	3
Retreat Centers	0000	S																P	P	P	P	P					P	3

P = USE BY RIGHT   D = DEVELOPMENT STANDARDS   S = SPECIAL USE PERMIT REQUIRED   Z = OVERLAY ZONING REQUIRED
* = INDICATES ADDITIONAL DISTRICT REQUIREMENTS SEE SECTION 30-4-5.3

30-4-33

A table of uses, like the one depicted above from the Greensboro, North Carolina, zoning ordinance, sets out whether each particular land use is permitted automatically, permitted under certain conditions, or prohibited in each zoning district (see key at bottom of table).

feet for each dwelling unit and may require the house to be located at least 50 feet from the front property line, 20 feet from the rear property line, and 10 feet from each side property line. In a different residential district the minimum lot size may be 20,000 square feet, with the same front, rear, and side yard setbacks. The ordinance may also establish minimum lot widths and a minimum street frontage for each lot. As a variation of these typical setback requirements, some zoning ordinances include what are in effect maximum setbacks in some zoning districts. For example, a commercial district may have a "build to" line, requiring all new stores to be no more than 20 feet from the street right-of-way.

Zoning standards for building dimensions also typically set maximum height and structural bulk limits. For example, a neighborhood commercial district may limit building height to no more than 35 feet and building square footage to 5,000 square feet or less, to cover no more than 50 percent of the lot area. While the use of minimum floor areas for residential structures is common in private restrictive covenants, only a few North Carolina zoning ordinances include minimum sizes for single-family homes. It is increasingly common for ordinances to have a maximum square footage for some residential districts to limit construction of houses that are far larger than the neighboring homes.

Increasingly various other dimensional standards are included in zoning ordinances. Some ordinances use a "floor area ratio" to regulate intensity of development, particularly in commercial areas. The floor area ratio is calculated by dividing the total square footage on all floors of a building on a lot by the square footage of the lot. For example, a 10,000 square foot lot with a 3,000 square foot building would have a floor area ratio of 0.3, while a 10,000 square foot lot with a multi-story building with a total floor area of 50,000 square feet would have a floor area ratio of 5.0. The ordinance would set different maximum floor area ratios for different zoning districts. Many ordinances limit the total amount of impervious surface coverage on a lot in order to manage stormwater runoff—for example, requiring that not more than 20 percent of a lot be covered by buildings and driveways.

Other Common Zoning Requirements

Land use and lot and building size limits provide the basis for a zoning ordinance, but modern zoning increasingly specifies other land development standards as well. Typical provisions include standards on landscaping, parking, signs, flood hazards, watershed protection, and historic preservation. Others include regulations regarding development timing and relating development approvals to availability of public services.

Landscape

Landscaping requirements typically apply to nonresidential land uses. For example, new businesses and industries may be required to have a planted buffer to provide a separation between uses or to assist in protecting water quality. Zoning ordinances may require provision of landscaping along the street front or in parking areas to enhance the community's appearance. The size of the area to be landscaped and even the type of plants may be specified.

Parking

In order to prevent street congestion or impositions on neighbors, ordinances usually require some land uses to provide a minimum amount of off-street parking on site. For example, a restaurant may be required to provide one parking place for each four seats provided, an office building may be required to provide one parking place for each 250 square feet of floor space in the building, and an industry may be required to provide two parking places for every three employees. The zoning ordinance will usually also specify the size of the parking places, whether they must be paved, where on the site they can be located, traffic flow within the parking area, and other site-design standards.

Signs

Zoning ordinances often include sign regulations, though sometimes a separate sign ordinance covers these regulations. Typical sign regulations include limits on location (for example, no billboards allowed in residential zoning districts and a minimum distance between billboards), size (maximum height and square footage), and types (for example, a prohibition on flashing lights, portable signs, or windblown signs). Regulation of signs raises some constitutional issues related to free speech that are discussed further in Chapter 15. There are also federal and state limits on how local governments may regulate billboards and other outdoor advertising signs, which are discussed in Chapter 14.

Flood Hazards

Many zoning ordinances include standards to reduce flood hazards. State and federal statutes do not mandate local zoning regulation of flood hazard areas, but they strongly encourage it and set some standards for any floodplain zoning that is adopted. Under federal law, property owners in a community are not eligible for federal flood insurance unless the local government has adopted floodplain zoning regulations that meet minimum federal standards. These standards generally prohibit development in the floodway, require elevation of the lowest habitable floor above the one-hundred-year flood level in the broader floodplain, and limit location of manufactured housing in the floodplain. Most every city and county with flood hazard areas therefore has a floodplain regulation, either as part of zoning or as a separate ordinance.

The state laws on flood hazard areas were updated after the devastating floods of Hurricane Floyd in 1999. These laws limit certain land uses in the flood hazard area (no solid or hazardous waste facilities, salvage yards, or chemical storage are permitted). State law also requires local governments to have an approved hazard mitigation plan and to be eligible for the national flood insurance program in order to receive state disaster assistance funds.

Water Quality

The state of North Carolina requires all local governments that have jurisdiction over land that drains into a public surface water supply to regulate development so as to minimize contamination of these lakes and rivers. State and federal regulations require that urban stormwater runoff be controlled to protect water quality in many areas. Such regulations limit the number of residential units per acre, limit the amount of built-on area in commercial or industrial areas, require vegetated buffers along the shoreline, and limit the placement of hazardous materials in these critical areas.

Design Standards and "Form-Based" Codes

Some zoning ordinances include design standards for individual buildings. These are most often applied in sensitive areas, such as downtowns and commercial corridors, and often only to nonresidential buildings. Historic district requirements that new buildings be consistent with the neigborhood's historic character are the most common form of design standards applicable to residential and nonresidential structures.

Design standards typically address elements commonly regulated in zoning, such as the height and bulk of buildings, their location on a lot, and the location of off-street parking. Some ordinances also address other aspects of building design, such as types of building materials, roof slope, and incorporation of architectural details into building façades. Many of these codes have a particular focus on the design of streets and public spaces, such as provisions for on-street parking, sidewalks, street trees, and the like.

A few jurisdictions have refocused their zoning to address the form and density of structures rather than the uses to which the buildings are devoted, employing a "form-based code" rather than a traditional zoning emphasis on land uses. It is increasingly common for jurisdictions to combine these two approaches using a "hybrid" ordinance that incorporates form-based standards for particular areas and more traditional use-based zoning in the remainder of the jurisdiction.

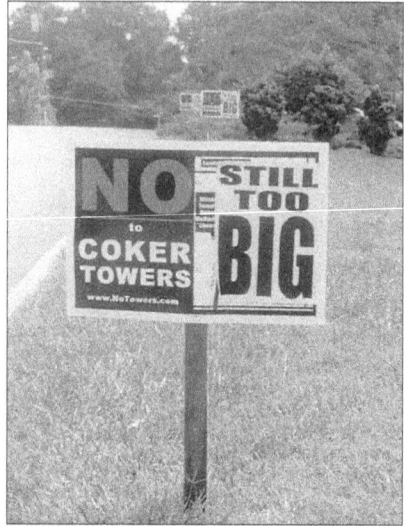

Zoning is often controversial. The sign at left objects to extension of zoning to rural portions of Watauga County. The sign at right urges the Raleigh City Council to use zoning to stop a proposed mixed-use development.

Zoning ordinances do not include construction standards for buildings or minimum habitability standards for residences. Construction is regulated through a uniform state building code and maintenance of residences for basic habitability is regulated through a housing code. See Chapter 5 for a brief discussion of these codes.

Notes

1. Village of Euclid v. Ambler Realty Co., 272 U.S. 365 (1926).

2. David W. Owens & Dayne Batten, *2012 Zoning Survey Report*, PLAN. & ZONING L. BULL. No. 20 (School of Government, July 2012). For a summary of the other land use regulations and a list of which local governments in North Carolina have adopted each, see DAVID W. OWENS & NATHAN BRANSCOME, AN INVENTORY OF LOCAL GOVERNMENT LAND USE ORDINANCES IN NORTH CAROLINA (Special Series No. 21, May 2006).

3. DAVID W. OWENS & ANDREW STEVENSON, AN OVERVIEW OF ZONING DISTRICTS, DESIGN STANDARDS, AND TRADITIONAL NEIGHBORHOOD DESIGN IN NORTH CAROLINA ZONING ORDINANCES (Special Series No. 25, Oct. 2007).

Chapter 5

Other Development Regulations

While local governments use zoning as their principal tool to regulate land use, additional ordinances are often used to regulate other aspects of development. The most commonly used additional ordinances are subdivision ordinances and building codes. A variety of other specialized ordinances affecting development may also be adopted.

In recent years an increasing number of local governments have attempted to simplify development regulation by consolidating zoning and other related ordinances into a single, unified development ordinance (often referred to as a UDO). The North Carolina statutes allow all development-related ordinances to be combined into this type of ordinance. A 2004 School of Government survey indicated about a quarter of North Carolina cities and counties had combined their development regulations into a UDO,[1] and more have done so since then. There has also been a move to develop common development regulations among neighboring jurisdictions, such as several contiguous cities and the county in which they are located all adopting a common zoning and development ordinance.

Although development regulations may be combined into a single UDO, the legal authority for each type of regulation is provided in separate statutory authorizations. While these may be separate sections of a single local ordinance, the statutory requirements and authority are tied to and limited by the separate statutory provisions.[2] For example, an exaction authorized by the subdivision statute can only be required when there is a qualifying subdivision, not for any approval mandated by the other sections of a UDO.

Subdivision Ordinances

A 2004 School of Government survey indicated 83 percent of responding cities (including almost all cities with populations over 5,000) and 88 percent of the state's counties had adopted a subdivision ordinance.[3] Subdivision control ordinances regulate the creation of new lots or separate parcels of land. Subdivision ordinances most typically address new residential developments but can also be applied to commercial, industrial, and mixed-use developments.

Subdivision ordinances serve a variety of purposes. They facilitate record keeping regarding land ownership by setting clear standards for surveying lots, marking them on the ground, and recording plat maps with the register of deeds. There are detailed state laws on surveying and mapping lots. A local plat review officer signs off on plats before they are recorded.

From a land use standpoint, subdivision ordinances usually include standards on the size and shape of new lots. They may include regulations concerning minimum street frontage or road access. Unlike zoning, however, a subdivision ordinance does not address what future use can be made of the lots that are created.

Another major aspect of most subdivision ordinances is the specification of standards regarding provision of common improvements, such as roads and utilities, and how they are to be laid out and constructed. The ordinance often includes detailed standards for these improvements, such as angles allowed for intersections, pavement standards for roads, and detailed engineering requirements for water and sewer lines. See Chapter 15 for a discussion of the scope of exactions that can be required.

State law exempts several types of land divisions from coverage by local subdivision ordinances. If all of the parcels created are greater than 10 acres and there are no new public streets being created, the subdivision is not subject to local regulation. Likewise, division of a tract of 2 acres or less into no more than three lots is exempt if there are no new public streets and all the lots meet or exceed the standards in the subdivision ordinance.

Unlike zoning, North Carolina statutes enabling local subdivision regulation do not set out any procedural requirements that must be followed in the plat review and approval process. Each city and county fashions its own review process. Local governments are free to create different classes of subdivisions (such as "major" subdivision and "minor" subdivisions) and use different review procedures based on those classifications. Nonetheless, a fairly typical approval process has emerged.

A preliminary *sketch plan* may be required as a first step. This is often reviewed by the planning staff to assure there are no glaring problems before the owner goes to the time and expense of preparing plats for the subsequent stages of approval. In some ordinances this step in the review process is encouraged but not required, while in others it is mandated.

The key decision in the subdivision approval process is usually the *preliminary plat.* Despite the name, there is little that is "preliminary" about this. The preliminary plat application usually requires detailed survey plats of all the lots and engineering details on all of the proposed and required improvements. The preliminary plat is widely circulated among various government agencies to assure compliance with standards within their area of expertise. For example, in cities the utilities department will check the water and sewer specifications, the transportation department will review proposed streets, and the fire department may check streets for acceptability for use by fire trucks and the adequacy of fire hydrant location. In counties, in addition to reviews by the planning staff, the preliminary plat is reviewed by the health department regarding acceptability for wells and septic tanks and by the state Department of Transportation for roads that will be dedicated to the state.

Since the reviews are generally technical reviews for compliance with objective standards, preliminary plat approval is usually a ministerial decision that does not require an evidentiary or public hearing. Preliminary plat approval is often assigned to the planning board or a staff technical review committee. Preliminary plat approval authorizes the owner to install the required public improvements and make other site improvements but does not authorize sale of the lots being created (although under carefully prescribed conditions it is permissible to enter into contracts for the future sale or lease of lots shown in an approved preliminary plat).

After the improvements are installed, the city or county inspects them for compliance with the ordinance. If they meet the standards and are built as proposed, *final plat approval* is given. Approval is required if the work is consistent with the terms of the ordinance and the preliminary plat approval. Although there is little discretion involved with final plat approval, this decision is often made by the city council or county board of commissioners. With final plat approval the city or county formally accepts the dedication of streets and utilities, allows the plat to be recorded with the register of deeds, and authorizes the owner to begin selling lots.

A local government must base its decision on subdivision approval only upon the standards for plat approval specifically set out in its ordinance. If the standards for decision are entirely objective (and that is the case with most subdivision ordinances), this is a ministerial or administrative decision. If standards that involve judgment and discretion are added (such as not having a significant adverse impact on traffic), then the decision is quasi-judicial and must follow those procedures (see Chapter 8).

Building and Housing Codes

Building codes regulate how new construction must be conducted. Building codes include detailed standards for structural safety and for electrical, plumbing, and heating systems.

In North Carolina all cities and counties are required by state law to enforce the North Carolina State Building Code. The building code addresses minimum design and construction issues, such as an adequate foundation, structural integrity, adequate insulation, and proper building materials. In addition to structural integrity, the building code sets minimum standards for a building's electrical, plumbing, and heating and air conditioning systems. There are separate codes for one- and two-family residential structures and for commercial, industrial, and multifamily buildings.

The building code is uniform throughout the state—each local government applies the code approved by the state Building Code Council and no local variations in the code are allowed. The state also sets standards for building inspectors. Each inspector must pass the appropriate state examination to be licensed to conduct particular types of inspections.

The approval process includes submission of plans for the structure to be built, issuance of a *building permit*, periodic inspections during the course of construction to assure adherence with each aspect of the code, and issuance of a *certificate of compliance* (often termed a certificate of occupancy or CO) at the conclusion of building to verify that all requirements have been met. State law specifies that building permits expire in six months if work is not commenced and expire if work is ceased for twelve months after it is commenced.

Housing codes set minimum standards for residential structures. For example, they may require a minimum square footage of space for each occupant, availability of adequate sanitary facilities, an adequate heating source, and avoidance of unsafe conditions (such as exposed wiring or holes in the floor).

Unlike building codes, housing codes are not mandatory in North Carolina. They are adopted at the option of each city and county. A 2004 School of Government survey indicated just over half of the cities and just over a quarter of the counties had adopted a housing code.[4]

Housing codes are often enforced on the basis of complaints received. Cities and counties with housing codes can order repairs to be made to substandard residential structures. Homes that are not repaired can be ordered to be closed or demolished. Some local governments coordinate housing code enforcement with various revitalization programs, such as financial assistance to low-income residents for home repairs.

In addition to building and housing codes, cities and counties may also adopt *maintenance codes* for nonresidential structures. These codes can set minimum standards of maintenance, sanitation, and safety, such as requiring repair of broken windows. If the owner abandons any intent to repair (shown by a failure to bring the structure up to code within two years for most buildings, five years for manufacturing facilities or industrial warehouses), the local government may order the structure to be repaired or demolished.

Historic Districts and Landmarks

Many zoning ordinances provide special coverage for historic neighborhoods and for particularly important individual historic landmark structures. North Carolina has a special statute allowing protection of these resources through zoning. As shown in Figure 5.1, the State Historic Preservation Office reported in 2010 that over 140 North Carolina cities and counties have or are participating in a historic preservation commission.

Zoning ordinances may place historic neighborhoods in a special zoning district in order to assure that future development is consistent with the character of the neighborhood. This is most often accomplished by creating a historic district overlay zone that establishes special review requirements in addition to the basic zoning that already applies. The restrictions require that a "certificate of appropriateness" be secured from the historic preservation commission for any new construction, for any alteration of the exteriors of existing buildings, and for any demolition or removal of a

Figure 5.1   Local Governments in North Carolina with Historic Preservation Commissions as of September 30, 2010

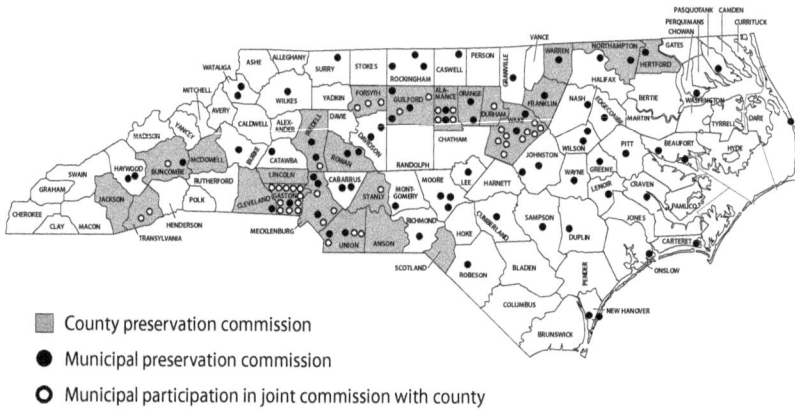

☐ County preservation commission

● Municipal preservation commission

○ Municipal participation in joint commission with county

structure. Similar protections can be established for individual buildings designated as historic landmarks.

The standards for securing a certificate of appropriateness must be set out in the ordinance and must generally relate to maintenance of the particular character of that individual neighborhood, what the statutes refer to as "congruity." Whether a particular project is "incongruous with the special character" of a historic district must be looked at contextually, considering the entire district. For example, a person would not be allowed to build a brick ranch in a neighborhood of Victorian homes or to build a Colonial-style home in a neighborhood of turn-of-the-century bungalows. These regulations can include a requirement stipulating that a permit to demolish a structure can be delayed for up to one year to allow time to develop a strategy for its preservation.

The zoning ordinance commonly provides for a historic preservation commission to develop and administer these rules. Such a commission must have at least three members, and members must have set terms of up to four years and must reside within the jurisdiction. A majority of the members must have some special expertise in historic preservation. Another citizen board, such as the planning board or community appearance board, can serve as this commission if at least three of its members have the required expertise. In addition to handling administrative responsibilities, these commissions can also acquire landmarks, restore and operate historic properties, and conduct educational programs.

In a departure from the usual rule that quasi-judicial decisions are appealed directly to superior court, appeals of decisions of a historic commission regarding certificates of appropriateness go to the board of adjustment. The board of adjustment, however, acts much like an appeals court in this particular situation. It does not conduct a new hearing; rather, it reviews the record established by the historic commission and determines if there was sufficient evidence to support the decision and whether the decision was arbitrary and capricious. If the parties want to contest the board of adjustment's decision, they can then appeal to superior court.

Development Timing—Moratoria and APFOs

Development regulations have also long considered the timing of development. The two most common tools used to address this are development moratoria and provisions tying development approval to the availability of adequate public facilities, such as roads, utilities, and schools.

Occasionally local governments need to place a temporary halt to development approvals. There may be an interest in preserving the status quo while a plan or ordinance is updated. There may be a need to develop new standards to address an emerging issue. Or there may be inadequate water, sewer, or road capacity to develop in a particular area. State law allows cities and counties to impose temporary moratoria on any required development approval. However, moratoria may not be applied to residential uses if the purpose of the moratorium is developing new plans or ordinances.

The duration of the moratorium must be reasonable in light of the specific conditions or issue that led to its imposition. At the time a moratorium is adopted the governing board must also adopt a statement addressing four points: (1) why the moratorium is being imposed and what alternatives were considered, (2) exactly what approvals are subject to the moratorium, (3) how long the moratorium will last and why that is a reasonable time period, and (4) what actions will be taken to address the problems that necessitated the moratorium and a schedule for their completion.

The process for adoption of a moratorium is the same as adoption of a zoning amendment (see Chapter 7). However, if the moratorium is needed

Can This Old Neighborhood Be Saved? The *A-S-P* Case

Raleigh's Oakwood neighborhood has a history similar to many downtown neighborhoods in North Carolina's cities and towns. This twenty-block area, located just northeast of the downtown business district, started as a prosperous residential area. A number of fine Victorian homes were built there between the Civil War and the turn of the century, interspersed with bungalows and other modest homes. However, as suburban growth exploded after the Great Depression, the neighborhood gradually declined. By the 1960s, most of the city's political and business leaders had long ago moved on to other neighborhoods, often replaced by absentee landlords who divided the large old homes into multiunit rental properties.

In the 1970s the future character of the neighborhood was uncertain. Some urban pioneers had begun revitalization efforts, but crime, proposed new highways, and physical deterioration of Oakwood's once grand homes were taking their toll. Local residents banded together to form the Society for the Preservation of Historic Oakwood to help save both individual structures and the neighborhood. They also sought state recognition and local zoning protection for their neighborhood.

In 1972 A-S-P Associates bought a dilapidated house in the neighborhood. The house was on a lot just behind the governor's mansion. The company demolished the house and in 1975 proposed to put up a modern office building. This seemed a reasonable proposition, since the lot had been zoned for office use since 1961 and the state medical society had recently constructed a modern office building a few lots down the block. Many of the residences in the area immediately west of the Oakwood neighborhood had already been demolished, many for the expanding state government complex. But another modern office building might further tip the neighborhood's future away from the revitalized residential area with a special character and feel.

Both the state and the city of Raleigh took regulatory steps to help the Oakwood neighborhood. The state nominated the neighborhood for inclusion on the National Register of Historic Places, and this designation was made in 1974. In 1975, after a year of study and discussion, the city designated the neighborhood as a historic district, creating an overlay zoning district that required new structures to have architectural styles compatible with the historic Victorian character of Oakwood.

A-S-P promptly sued the city, challenging the validity of historic district rules. North Carolina had a long line of court cases stating that, while aesthetics could be considered in zoning, they could not be the sole basis of a regulation. In 1979, however, the state supreme court rejected A-S-P's arguments, adjusted its course, and upheld the city's regulations.[a] The court held that properly studied and framed historic district regulations advance the public welfare in a variety of important ways and a requirement that new structures not be "incongruous" with the historic aspects of the district is legally acceptable.

So what happened on this lot? An office building was indeed eventually built there. However, as the photo below illustrates, this was not a typical modern office building. The structure was built in the style of the Victorian homes typical of the Oakwood neighborhood, a much more "congruous" result than the original proposal. Many additional homes in the neighborhood have been restored, and Oakwood has a residential vitality that was almost lost. In fact, the legislature in 2003 approved a plan to sell the large homes in Oakwood that had been purchased and converted to state

This structure was eventually built on the A-S-P site.

offices, with the homes being returned to residential use and the proceeds going into a fund for the maintenance of the historic governor's mansion. This plan also includes construction of new housing on the lots that had been cleared and turned into parking lots.

---

a. A-S-P Assocs. v. City of Raleigh, 298 N.C. 207 (1979).

to address an imminent and substantial threat to public health and safety, no public hearing is required. Also, if the duration of the moratorium is sixty days or less, a public hearing is required but only one published notice of the hearing is required. That notice must be published at least seven days prior to the hearing.

Several types of approvals are not subject to moratoria absent a threat to public health and safety. Development moratoria do not apply to projects that have secured a vested right (see Chapter 13). A moratorium also does not apply to applications for preliminary or final plat approval or to applications for special or conditional use permits if, in both instances, a completed application has been accepted for review prior to the call for a public hearing on the moratorium.

Adequate public facility ordinances (APFOs) tie development approval to the availability of essential public facilities. These requirements are sometimes incorporated into a zoning or unified development ordinance and are sometimes adopted as a separate ordinance. Under an APFO, development is not permitted at a particular site unless and until a defined level of public services is available. A fully developed APFO requires adoption of a long-term capital improvement program and then sequences development approvals as the required facilities become available. While this type of ordinance is common in many high-population growth states, a simpler approach is typically used in North Carolina. This alternative requires an analysis of facility availability and development impacts, with individual development approvals allowed only where adequate public facilities are available and denied where the project would lead to a degradation of facilities.

The authority to regulate on the basis of adequacy of public facilities is not, however, the same as authority to impose impact fees, which are used by some local governments to address projected deficiency in public facility capacity. Impact fees are assessments on the owners or developers of land made by local governments to recoup some or all of the capital costs of public facilities needed to serve new development. About half of the states authorize broad use of impact fees, rather than general tax revenues, to finance the new roads, utilities, fire stations, parks, schools, and other public facilities necessitated by new development.

North Carolina local governments have authority to impose fees for a variety of "public enterprise" functions, such as the provision of water and sewer services. The zoning and subdivision statutes also allow regulations to require land dedication, construction, or payment of fees to address the specific public facility needs of new development, such as internal roads, utilities, parks, and community service facilities. But only those fees and exactions expressly authorized by the statutes may be imposed. See the section entitled "Taking" in Chapter 15 for a discussion of the constitutional limits on exactions and similar requirements.

Other Specialized Ordinances

Many local governments adopt a variety of other ordinances to regulate particular aspects of development. Some cities and counties adopt these as sections of their zoning ordinances, some incorporate them as chapters in a UDO, while still others have separate ordinances for each subject. Chapter 14 sets out the statutory limits for a number of these specialized ordinances.

A common type of specialized ordinance are those designed to prevent one person's use of land from harming their neighbors. *Nuisance lot* ordinances set minimum standards to prevent lots from becoming overgrown or repositories for unsightly and unhealthy collections of refuse. *Junk car* and *abandoned car* ordinances limit keeping inoperable vehicles on a site. The state has specific statutes that set the contours and enforcement procedures for these ordinances.

Other ordinances set standards for typical land uses (and are particularly common in unzoned areas). *Mobile home park* ordinances often set standards for lot size, density, and internal street width and paving where there are a specified number of adjacent manufactured home sites under common ownership or management. *Sign* ordinances set specifications on what types of signs are allowed and may include standards on their size, height, or illumination. *Junkyard* ordinances often set standards for fencing and security and limit large collections of junk or junked cars in inappropriate locations. *Adult entertainment* ordinances often set both location standards (typically minimum separations from each other and from sensitive land uses) and operational standards (such as limits on hours of operation, open-booth requirements, lighting standards, and licensing of employees and owners). *Telecommunication tower* ordinances set standards for the location, height, and design of and fencing around towers needed to support wireless telecommunications.

Still other ordinances protect natural resources. *Sedimentation control* ordinances regulate construction sites to keep soil from eroding. *Stormwater control* ordinances set minimum standards for retention of stormwater on site and its controlled release to avoid contamination of surface waters. *Flood hazard* ordinances limit construction in floodways and set minimum construction standards for structures in the wider floodplain (such as elevation of the lowest habitable floor above the 100-year flood level). *Tree protection* ordinances limit the removal of large trees and set standards for landscaping cut-over areas.

Restrictive Covenants

In addition to land use restrictions imposed by government, private agreements such as restrictive covenants or deed restrictions can limit how land is used. For example, the developer of a new residential subdivision may establish restrictive covenants that set a minimum size for houses, limit architectural styles, or restrict where recreational vehicles may be stored on a lot. Such covenants are often more strict than local development regulations.

For the most part these restrictive covenants are legal and enforceable. There are limits to restrictive covenants, as they must not violate state law or public policy. An example of an illegal covenant would be one that restricts sale of a house to buyers of a certain race.

The enforcement of restrictive covenants is a private matter and the local government is generally not involved. If a landowner feels someone is violating the covenants, he or she can sue that person to compel compliance. The city or county, however, does not cite that person for a violation of city or county ordinances. If the zoning ordinance and restrictive covenants conflict, the rule is that the more restrictive provision is controlling (but again, the government only enforces the ordinance requirement and the private owners enforce the covenant requirements).

Notes

1. DAVID W. OWENS & NATHAN BRANSCOME, AN INVENTORY OF LOCAL GOVERNMENT LAND USE ORDINANCES IN NORTH CAROLINA 5–6 (Special Series No. 21, May 2006).

2. Lanvale Properties, LLC v. Cnty. of Cabarrus, 366 N.C. 449 (2012).

3. OWENS & BRANSCOME, *supra* note 1, at 4.

4. *Id.* at 5.

Chapter 6

Administration

City and county staff play a vital role in the day-to-day administration of local planning and development regulations programs. The staff is responsible for processing routine permit applications, providing support to the various citizen boards involved, maintaining accurate records, and handling enforcement. Much of this work is done by the zoning administrator and inspectors (collectively called zoning officers). Planners, clerks, and other office personnel also play important roles, but the focus of this chapter is on the staff members who issue permits, make site inspections, and handle enforcement actions.

Administrators and Officers

Each zoning and other development regulatory ordinance should specify who has responsibility for ordinance administration, designating a city or county staff position as the administrator. In the absence of a specific designation in the zoning or other ordinance, the city or county manager assigns that responsibility to a particular person or group of persons.

The statutes allow substantial flexibility in just where that responsibility is housed. In most local governments in North Carolina, this responsibility is assigned to an inspections department, although it can be assigned to a planning department or some other department within the city or county government. Some smaller cities contract with another local government or a private contractor to provide these administrative services. Counties and several cities also have the option of setting up a joint inspections and enforcement department.

The administrator is a public officer of the local government and, as an "officer" instead of an "employee," has certain powers, duties, and protections. The administrator must take an oath of office, swearing or affirming to support the constitution and laws and to faithfully carry out his or her duties. Officers working under the administrator also have decision-making authority and must take an oath of office. The oath of office is administered at the time the officer assumes his or her duties. It should not be confused with the oath to testify truthfully that is administered each time the officer presents testimony in a hearing.

Duties of Officers

Zoning and other administrative and enforcement officers have a number of important duties. They process all applications (see Figure 6.1). They explain the ordinance requirements to the public, make application forms available, and review applications to verify the information provided and assess the application's compliance with the terms of the zoning ordinance. Officers issue all routine permits. If an application involves both fact-finding and the application of discretionary standards, such as with a conditional use permit or a special use permit, the decision must be made by a citizen board rather than a staff member (see Chapter 8 for details on the process for these quasi-judicial zoning decisions).

Officers are also responsible for making interpretations of the ordinances and issuing determinations as to zoning compliance. Different legal consequences stem from sending a letter with general advice as distinguished from a formal determination. A zoning administrator should explicitly state in a letter whether it is a nonbinding "zoning verification" letter (such as one merely stating what the current zoning of a parcel is and verifying the list of permitted uses) or a final, binding "zoning determination." While not required, a formal determination often includes a statement on how and when the decision can be appealed.

Figure 6.1   Zoning Clearance for Building Permit Application

ZONING CLEARANCE FOR BUILDING PERMIT APPLICATION

GENERAL INFORMATION

Job Address_____   Tax Map No._____

Owner _____   Zoning_____

Flood Plain_____

Contractor_____   Contact Person_____

Address _____   Phone Number_____

Lincense No. _____   Priv. License_____   Sq. Ft._____

Type of Application: _____addition _____new construction _____other

Estimated Cost_____

SPECIFIC ZONING REQUIREMENTS

	MIN	ACTUAL		MIN	ACTUAL
Lot Size	____	____	Parking Spaces		
Lot Width	____	____	# Spaces	____	____
Setbacks:			Handicapped	____	____
Front Yard	____	____			
Rear Yard	____	____			
Right Yard	____	____	Signs		
Left Yard	____	____	Ground	____	____
			Flush Mounted	____	____
Minimum Combined Side Yard	____	____			
% of Lot Coverage	____	____			

REQUIRED INFORMATION (must be submitted to the Inspections Department when making application for a building permit along with 3 sets of complete building plans) and an approved erosion control plan, if greater than one (1) acre.
_____ Site Plan Showing:

_____ Lot Dimensions		_____	Easements
_____ Structure Size & Location		_____	Parking Layout
_____ Set Backs		_____	Flood Elevation Certification
_____ Front Yard		_____	Number of Employees
_____ Rear Yard		_____	Other (specify)
_____ Left Yard		_____	Erosion Control Plan
_____ Right Yard			(approved by North Carolina NRCD)

_____   _____
Signature of Applicant   Zoning Officer

pg 26

THIS FORM AND ABOVE REQUIRED INFORMATION MUST BE PRESENTED TO THE INSPECTION DEPARTMENT

Zoning and other administrative and enforcement officers process a number of applications. These include verification that the zoning ordinance has been complied with (sample application form above is from the City of Statesville, North Carolina), sign permits, special and conditional use permits, variances, rezoning requests, and many others.

Local governments should follow a standardized process when making formal staff determinations. A few guidelines for this process follow.

1. When drafting formal interpretations, an administrator should seek input and advice of other professionals within the jurisdiction, particularly from the city or county attorney. Interpretation of the ordinance is a duty assigned to the zoning administrator; he or she must make the decision, but input from others is often helpful.

2. Notice of the decision should be promptly provided to all persons directly affected by the decision. State law requires written notice to the owner of the property subject to the decision (and to the party requesting the decision if that was not the owner). The written notice can be delivered by first class mail, email, or personal delivery. Since an appeal to the board of adjustment must be made within thirty days of receipt of the decision, it is important to let those with appeal rights know of the decision and when the clock for appeals has started to run.

   Both neighbors who are directly affected and the local government also have rights of appeal, so some system of providing prompt notice of formal zoning determinations to the petitioner, the neighbors, the city or county manager, and the governing board should be in place. A landowner who receives a determination may post a notice on the site that a determination has been made, thereby providing notice of the decision to the neighbors and starting the clock for making an appeal to the board of adjustment.

3. Since binding interpretations and determinations have long-term effect, there should be a system of logging, tracking, and maintaining them. Future staff members and the public need to know what determinations have been made. Some local governments add interpretative annotations to the ordinance, while others keep more informal records. Whatever system is used, it clearly needs to be more systematic and formal than relying on the memory of zoning administrators that the record of a determination is "somewhere in the files."

Officers are responsible for making inspections during and at the conclusion of the permitted work to assure that ordinance requirements have been met. Officers investigate complaints and initiate enforcement actions when violations are discovered (see the more detailed discussion of enforcement below).

Officers also often perform routine tasks for the planning board and board of adjustment, including preparing reports, assuring proper notice of meetings, and reporting on cases. The city or county clerk and the planning staff often share responsibility for these administrative duties. Some boards request staff recommendations on individual cases, while other boards ask the staff to report only the facts of the case. Either approach is legally acceptable.

Administrators are also responsible for maintaining all appropriate records. Files must be maintained on all applications and permit decisions. Records of enforcement actions and decisions by boards on permits, appeals, variances, and ordinance changes must be maintained. These materials are public records and must be made available for public inspection during normal business hours.

The professionalism and demeanor of officers is a critical element in the successful implementation of development regulations. As former Institute of Government faculty member Phil Green noted, if the administrator "is energetic, imaginative, intelligent, sensitive, and calm, he will carry out the objectives of the ordinance with a minimum of misunderstanding, contention, and bad public relations. On the other hand, inattention to detail, lack of dedication, or arrogance can ensure that he and his fellow officers remain in constant hot water."[1]

Fees

Cities and counties routinely charge application and other administrative fees. A fee is usually required to request a rezoning; apply for a special or conditional use permit, a driveway permit, or a sign permit; file a variance petition; request approval of a subdivision plat; and so forth.

For the most part, the statutes are silent on the topic of fees in the administration of development regulations. The North Carolina Supreme Court concluded that reasonable fees can be required to offset these costs.[2] Fees are limited, however. They must be reasonable and generally not exceed the cost of the regulatory program. An administrative fee can recoup the costs of advertising and holding a hearing, staff analysis, and the like. If a fee moves beyond cost recovery, it is a tax, not an administrative fee.

Therefore, in setting the amount of these application fees, some staff analysis of actual costs should be made. Some local governments set the fee amount to recover all direct expenses, such as the cost of the newspaper advertisement of a hearing and required mailings. Others also recover the costs of staff time for review and analysis and reasonable overhead expenses. If the fee amount exceeds direct expenses, staff analysis should document typical costs.

Sliding fee scales, such as basing the fee on the number of lots or acreage involved in an application, should be used with caution. Higher fees charged for larger projects must not exceed the actual administrative costs of review, even if that project seemingly has a greater "ability to pay."

A local government can also pass some administrative costs directly on to the applicant without making them part of the application fee. For example, the ordinance may require that a traffic impact analysis or engineering verification of stormwater controls be submitted for certain types of applications. In these situations local governments often provide a list of approved contractors, and the applicant hires someone from that list. As long as the required information and analysis are needed for application review, the local government may require that the applicant pay for the study.

Good public policy might suggest that a local government consider the implications of who pays these administrative costs. That is, what portion of the actual costs should be borne by the applicant benefited by a potential approval and what portion by the taxpayers benefited by a review? A local government can set administrative fees to secure 100 percent cost recovery, 50 percent cost recovery, or some other proportion. This is a policy choice for the governing board. Legally, however, the applicant's share cannot be more than a reasonable estimate of actual costs.

Enforcement

The first step in enforcement is inspection of potential violations. Inspections are usually triggered by citizen complaints, but the staff may also conduct routine inspections.

An officer must have the permission of the landowner to go onto private property to inspect areas that cannot be viewed from public areas. If there are reasonable grounds to believe there may be a violation and permission is not granted, an officer can obtain an administrative search warrant from a magistrate or judge that will authorize a reasonable inspection (see Figure 6.2). An officer may enter a commercial establishment or any other area to which the public is invited without a warrant to make an initial investigation. However, if there is a need subsequently to gather more detailed evidence in a way that would not be expected of the usual customer (such as taking a number of photographs and measurements of a potential violation), an administrative search warrant must be obtained. If permission for such a detailed inspection is given without a warrant, many officers ask the person giving approval to sign a form authorizing the inspection to document that permission was in fact given.

If the officer determines that there has been a violation of an ordinance, enforcement action is initiated. Many local governments initially provide oral notice of the violation and allow a brief period for the owner to come into compliance. Formal enforcement action is commenced by sending a written notice of violation to the owner of the property. Notice may also be sent to the occupant if that is a different person. This notice of violation identifies the nature of the violation and directs the owner to bring the site into compliance within a set time.

If the officer determines that there is work under way that is in substantial violation of the ordinance or that is dangerous, the officer can issue a formal stop work order (see Figure 6.3). A stop work order must be in writing; it must specify the violation found; and it must tell the person what he or she must do to be able to resume work. Stop work orders can be appealed to the board of adjustment.

The officer also has the option of revoking any permits that are being violated, whether or not a stop work order has been issued. A permit revocation must be in writing and it can be appealed to the board of adjustment. The statutes provide that a building permit *must* be revoked in three instances: (1) when there is a substantial departure from approved plans, (2) when there is a failure to comply with the zoning ordinance, or (3) when there are false statements on the application. A permit *may* be revoked if it was mistakenly issued.

Figure 6.2   Administrative Inspection Warrant

After presenting an affidavit to a judge or magistrate setting forth the reasons to believe a violation exists, an officer can be issued an administrative search warrant, pictured above. It authorizes a reasonable inspection during regular business hours. The inspection must be made within forty-eight hours of the issuance of the warrant. Other warrants are available for periodic inspections, such as those done over the continuing course of construction.

Figure 6.3 Stop Work Order

DURHAM CITY-COUNTY
INSPECTIONS DEPARTMENT
101 CITY HALL PLAZA
DURHAM, N.C. 27701
(919) 560-4144
FAX 560-4484

STOP WORK ORDER

To:

Re:

In accordance with the authority contained in the North Carolina
State Building Code (Section 2.3 of Volume I-A and Section R-107.3
of Volume VII), as well as G.S. 153A-361 and G.S. 160A-421 of the
North Carolina General Statutes, you are hereby ordered to stop all
_____ work immediately on the structure at
the above referenced address.

This order is being issued because _____
_____. Work may not proceed until
_____.

                              Sincerely,

                              Code Enforcement Official

Received By: _____

Witnessed By: _____

Date: _____

AN EQUAL OPPORTUNITY/AFFIRMATIVE ACTION EMPLOYER

An official can issue a stop work order to halt construction on a project that is in violation of a development regulation.

Following the notice of violation, local governments have three additional legal tools for enforcement.

1. *Civil penalties.* If the local ordinance specifically authorizes civil penalties for violations, the local administrator may assess such a penalty. The amount of the civil penalty must be no more than an amount reasonably related to the amount of harm caused by the violation and the cost to the local government of securing compliance. The ordinance can provide that each day of continuing violation after notice of violation is a separate offense. The assessment of a civil penalty can be appealed to the board of adjustment.

2. *Criminal prosecution.* Violation of a local development ordinance is a misdemeanor and can be prosecuted as a criminal offense. State law makes violation of a local ordinance a misdemeanor, punishable by a fine of up to $200 as specified in the ordinance. (The maximum fine is $50 if the ordinance does not specify a higher amount.) If the person has five or more prior convictions, the sentence may include a jail term of up to twenty days. Many local governments have decriminalized their development regulations, explicitly removing criminal sanctions as a possible remedy for these violations.

3. *Injunctions or court orders.* The local government can seek an injunction or court order to compel compliance. To secure an injunction, the city or county must first file a lawsuit that asks a judge to take this action to order compliance. This kind of suit is usually used only in very serious cases, such as where the violation presents a threat to public health or safety or the other enforcement tools have been tried and have failed to secure compliance. Violation of a court order to comply subjects the violator to contempt of court sanctions, which can be severe—a violator may be held in jail until compliance is secured.

The decision on whether to initiate an enforcement action is left to the discretion and judgment of the administrator. Officers do have a duty to make a reasonable investigation of credible complaints, but there is no mandate that any particular enforcement action must result from an investigation. The fact that a similar prior violation by someone else has not been prosecuted is not a valid defense on the part of a person charged with a violation. Only in extreme instances—where there is conscious and intentional discrimination rather than laxity of enforcement—would selective enforcement be a valid defense to an alleged violation.

If officers do investigate and discover a violation but then there is a considerable delay before any enforcement action is taken, the courts have the option of refusing to allow enforcement. If the length of the delay is unreasonable and the delayed enforcement would put the violator at an unreasonable disadvantage, a court can find the intentionally delayed enforcement unfair and thus invalid.

Occasionally code enforcement officers must deal with closing or demolishing dilapidated or dangerous structures. Detailed statutory procedures must be followed in these cases. While the process varies depending on exactly which type of code violation is involved, these procedures generally require notice to the owner of the need for action, an administrative hearing before the code enforcement officer, and an opportunity for the owner to make repairs. If the violation is based on a housing code violation or the unsafe buildings statute, this hearing is quasi-judicial. If the owner fails to comply with an order to repair or demolish the offending structure, the governing board may authorize staff to take remedial action under some of these ordinances.

Liability

Administrative officers have immunity from suits related to carrying out their official duties. An officer does not have personal financial liability for good-faith mistakes made in carrying out his or her duties. Liability for officers is limited to intentional wrongdoing (such as assaulting an applicant); corrupt and malicious acts (such as intentionally denying a permit solely because of a personal vendetta against the applicant); or negligence in carrying out routine, nondiscretionary acts (such as running through a stoplight and causing an accident while driving to a site to conduct an inspection). There may also be personal liability if an officer is acting outside the scope of the officer's authority (such as using an officer's official position for personal financial gain rather than carrying out governmental duties).

The local government unit is also generally immune from liability based on the officer's actions. The government's immunity can be waived by the purchase of liability insurance, something many North Carolina cities and counties have done. The waiver is, however, limited to the amount of insurance coverage purchased by the local government.

Notes

1. Philip P. Green Jr., Legal Responsibilities of the Local Zoning Administrator in North Carolina 1 (2d ed. 1987).

2. Homebuilders Ass'n of Charlotte v. City of Charlotte, 336 N.C. 37 (1994).

Chapter 7

Adoption and Amendment of Land Development Regulations

State statutes set detailed procedures local governments must follow when they decide to consider adopting any land development regulation. Additional procedures must be followed when a zoning ordinance is involved. For the most part these same procedures must also be followed for all ordinance amendments or if the ordinance is proposed to be repealed (or an individual amendment rescinded).

As communities grow and change, they often find their zoning ordinance does not adequately address emerging issues or new development proposals. Thus many local governments are faced with the prospect of amending their zoning ordinances. There may be a need to add, update, or change the standards included in the requirements of the zoning text, such as adding siting requirements for telecommunications towers, amending setbacks along major streets, or revising off-street parking requirements. Frequently there are requests to rezone a parcel of land, amending the zoning map for that parcel. In some cases, the city or county may have acquired new territory that has to be zoned. Other ordinances must also be periodically updated, such as modernizing the road construction standards in a subdivision ordinance.

Basis for Rules

The special rules discussed in this chapter apply to all such legislative decisions, from the initial adoption of an ordinance to its amendment or entire repeal. Since more than 650 existing zoning ordinances have already been adopted in the state, and total repeal is almost unheard of, most of the discussion in this chapter focuses on amendments.

When local governing boards adopt or change a development regulation, they should expect scrutiny—even controversy. Packed public hearings, numerous phone calls, letters, visits, and high emotions will be standard fare. Such public response is understandable—a rezoning can, for example, affect many properties and lives. Local governing boards are wise to carefully consider the policy and legal aspects of changes as they consider these proposed changes in their ordinances.

The staff, planning board, and governing board should carefully evaluate the policy implications of a proposed ordinance amendment. Is the change consistent with the adopted plan for the area? What impact will it have on public services such as roads, schools, police, fire, water, and sewer? What impact will it have on the property owners and the neighbors? What policy precedent does it set for future requests for amendments? Local government officials should carefully discuss and consider these matters before they amend a development ordinance.

State law requires special procedures to be followed whenever these ordinances are adopted, amended, or repealed. These procedures help ensure that the local government follows a careful, deliberate decision-making process with broad notice and opportunity for public participation. For rezonings (zoning map amendments), the required procedures also ensure that those most directly affected by zoning ordinances—the landowners and immediate neighbors—have individual direct notice of the proposed rezoning and a full opportunity to make their views known.

Several kinds of special requirements for zoning amendments are discussed in this chapter. They include requirements for giving notice of the proposed legislative zoning decision to affected persons, for holding public hearings, and for requiring rezonings to be approved by a special majority vote if a valid protest petition has been filed. These requirements are contained in state law and apply to all zoning ordinances, unless the General Assembly makes a special amendment in state law at the request of a particular city or county. Individual ordinances may contain other requirements, added at the discretion of the local governing board. While a local government cannot adopt requirements that are contrary to or less demanding than state requirements, it may add supplemental or more demanding requirements. For example, many zoning ordinances add a requirement for a minimum waiting period between reviews of rezoning petitions for the same site. If these additional requirements are included in a particular ordinance, they are binding and must be followed.

Consideration of Ordinance Amendments
Initiation
The first question with amending development ordinances is, Who can start the process? Who can petition the city or county to amend the ordinance text or rezone a parcel?

The short answer is that any citizen can ask his or her local government to amend its development ordinances. Perhaps the most common type of amendment is a change in the zoning map. Rezoning petitions most often arise when a landowner asks for a change in zoning to accommodate a new development proposal. Sometimes a rezoning is proposed by an elected official, the planning board, or the staff. Or a neighborhood group or other interested citizens may propose a change. Though some zoning ordinances purport to limit requests for rezonings to those from a landowner or a local government body, such limitations are of dubious legality. Since anyone can petition the government for a change in its ordinances, anyone should be allowed to request a zoning map amendment.

While anyone can make a request, a city or county can impose some screening of petitions to determine which ones to send through the full review process. Many local governments send all petitions through a public hearing, planning board review, and vote by the board. But it is permissible to terminate the consideration of a proposed amendment prior to a hearing if that is the governing board's decision (and such a screening procedure is set out in the ordinance).

It is also permissible to charge a fee to any person proposing an ordinance amendment. The amount of the fee must be reasonable and must not exceed the administrative costs to the government, such as advertising the hearing and otherwise considering the request.

Waiting Periods

Rezoning an area involves substantial work for a number of parties. The owner usually prepares a petition requesting the change; the city or county staff must undertake a technical review of the proposal; the planning board and governing board must carefully consider and rule on the proposal; neighbors generally monitor the proposal and attend hearings to present their concerns; and members of the public often present their concerns about the future development of their community.

State statutes do not require a waiting period prior to consideration of a second petition to rezone the same parcel of land. Unless the local zoning ordinance provides one, an owner can come back to the city council or county board of commissioners as often and as soon as he or she wishes. However, because rezoning involves so much time, effort, and money, most local zoning ordinances require a waiting period before a second rezoning proposal for that land can be considered. For example, a local zoning ordinance may provide that if a rezoning proposal is denied, no other rezonings will be considered for that property for a period of six months, a year, or even two years. This helps prevent the waste of public and private resources spent on repetitious reviews of the same project. If the zoning ordinance includes a mandatory waiting period, it is binding and must be observed. These waiting periods for legislative zoning decisions do not apply to quasi-judicial decisions. In the absence of changed circumstances, a special use permit that has been denied may not be resubmitted no matter how much time has passed (see Chapter 8 for more details).

Legislative Hearings

Notice of Hearings

All amendments to a development ordinance require a public hearing. There are several ways citizens can be notified of the mandated public hearing on a proposed ordinance amendment. While a local government can always use as many notification tools as it desires, state law establishes four mandatory steps.

The first requirement is for *published notice*. There must be at least two newspaper advertisements of the public hearing on all development ordinance amendments. This applies both to amendments to the text of an ordinance and to rezonings (amendments of the zoning map). The advertisements must be run in a newspaper of general circulation in the area affected. Publication in a property owners' newsletter or a free advertising paper is allowed, but these will not count as the required published notice. Ads may be published in the legal ads section of the newspaper, though some cities and counties use larger (and more expensive) display advertisements. The first of the two notices must be published at least ten days, but not more than twenty-five days, before the hearing. The second notice must appear in a separate calendar week.

The content of the published notice should include a brief description of the subject of the hearing; the date, time, and location of the hearing; and a contact source for more detailed information. The full text of an amendment need not be included, but the explanation of the action being considered should have enough detail to allow an interested person to understand the nature of the proposal.

The second requirement is for *mailed notice*. Property owners most directly affected by a zoning map amendment—a rezoning—must get individual mailed notice of the hearing. This notice goes to the owners of all abutting property as well as property to be rezoned. The notice must be mailed to whoever is identified by the county tax records as the owner. An updated title search to determine whether the property has changed hands since the tax listing is not required. This notice may be sent by first-class mail (it does not have to be sent by registered or certified mail, though the local government may do so). A city or county may require someone proposing a rezoning to compile the list of owners who get this mailed notice, although the staff usually does the actual mailing. The mailing must be made at least ten days, but not more than twenty-five days, prior to the hearing. The mailing should notify the recipients of the proposed rezoning and the time and place of the hearing. A common practice is to mail the same notice used for the published notice. The city or county staff should maintain a copy of the mailing, a list of whom it went to, and a certification by the person making the mailing as to when it was done. The mailing is conclusively presumed to be valid if that certification is made unless there is a showing of fraud. A hearing notice must also be sent by certified mail (or other means that will provide actual notice) to the base commander for any proposed amendments that involve the following within five miles of a military base: a rezoning, changing permitted land uses, a telecommunication tower

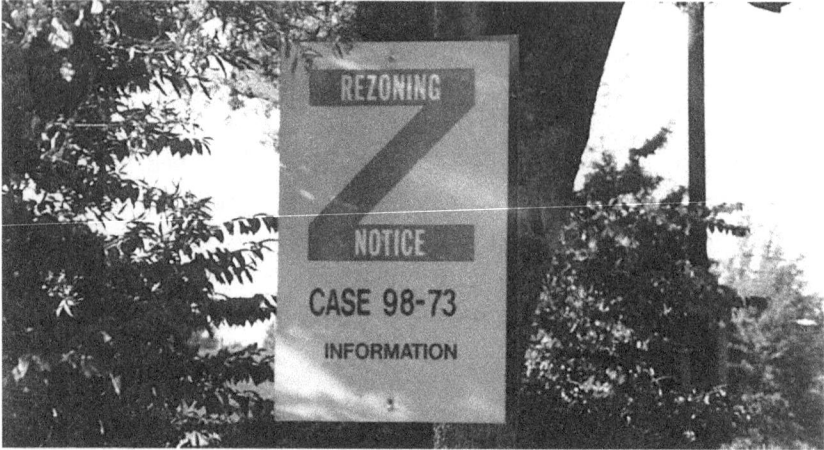

State law requires posting signs to advertise rezoning hearings.

or windmill, or a provision for a new major subdivision or a substantial enlargement of an existing subdivision.

The third requirement is for *posted notice*. A notice of the hearing on any proposed zoning map amendment must be posted on the affected site. Each local government has discretion as to the number and size of the signs and the timing of the mandatory posting, so long as the posting provides reasonable notice to interested persons. The statutes likewise do not mandate the content of the sign. Wording such as "Zoning Hearing Notice" is sufficient, along with contact information (such as a phone number for the city or county planning office) to obtain details about the hearing or proposed action.

The fourth requirement is for *actual notice*. If a rezoning is initiated by someone other than the owner of the property affected or by the local government, the landowner must be provided actual notice of the hearing. This notice can be accomplished by personal delivery or by a mailing that verifies receipt.

Where large-scale rezonings are involved—those affecting more than fifty parcels with at least fifty different landowners—cities and counties have the option of using an expanded published notice instead of individual mailed notices. With this alternative, the local government must run two half-page newspaper ads for the hearing (with the same timing as the regular published notice), post a notice of the hearing on the site, and mail letters to those property owners who live outside the newspaper's area of circulation. Given the high cost of complying with these requirements, this option is not used very often.

An individual ordinance can establish notice requirements in addition to those required by state law. Any such additional requirements are binding and must be observed. The most common of these require that mailed notices of hearings on rezonings be sent to all landowners within a specified distance of the proposed rezoning (such as all owners within 500 feet).

If the hearing notice requirements above are not strictly followed, any action the local government takes to amend the ordinance will be invalidated if the action is challenged in court. For the most part, any legal challenge to irregular procedures in ordinance adoption or amendment must be filed within three years of the challenged action.

Conduct of Hearings

Local governments can use a variety of forums to gather public comment on proposed ordinance amendments. Informal neighborhood meetings, meetings with interested groups, planning board hearings, and formal public hearings by the governing board are all frequently used to solicit comments. Most such meetings are optional, and it is up to each local government to decide which kind is appropriate.

However, state law does set a minimum threshold—the governing board must hold at least one formal public hearing before adopting, amending, or repealing a development ordinance. (Special legislation allows planning boards in a few North Carolina communities to run such hearings; some zoning ordinances provide for a joint hearing by the planning board and the governing board.) Not every amendment petition must get a public notice and hearing, however. Some local governments allow the planning board to screen out some petitions. But in order for the petition ultimately to be adopted, it must have gone through these public notice and hearing requirements.

A formal legislative public hearing on proposed amendments is a chance for citizens to make their views known directly to the governing board. Because a legislative public hearing is not an evidentiary hearing, there is no need to have sworn testimony. (Evidentiary hearings are required for appeals, variances, and special and conditional use permits and are discussed in Chapter 8). Citizens are free to offer their personal opinions and views in the hearing and to lobby board members before and after the hearing. The board need not make any formal findings of fact at the conclusion of the hearing (though a written statement briefly setting out the board's rationale for its decision on any zoning amendment is required). The motives of the board in making a decision are generally irrelevant unless a clearly impermissible motive, such as racial discrimination, is present.

Even with this latitude, it is important that these legislative hearings be conducted fairly. Reasonable rules may be established to limit the number of speakers, the amount of time each speaker is given, and the overall length of the hearing. The governing board is not obligated to allow everyone present to speak. Speakers can also be required to limit their remarks to the subject of the hearing. Local governments should have clear, fair policies on these points and make the policies available to all concerned persons. Policies beyond time limits for individual speakers should probably include procedures for the selection of speakers. For example, many cities and counties have a sign-up sheet available prior to the start of the hearing and take speakers in the order of sign-up. Some provision also needs to be made to assure that proponents of one side of a controversial issue are not allowed to monopolize the hearing to the exclusion of opposing points of view. Ideally these policies should be adopted and distributed well before a controversial hearing occurs, but at a minimum they should be announced and explained at the outset of the hearing.

A copy of the proposed amendment should be available for public review at the time the notice of hearing is provided. Usually the proposed amendment is posted on the local government's website and a paper copy is made available at the government's office for public review.

Rehearings

Must an additional hearing be held if the governing board decides to make changes in the proposed action after the public hearing? For example, if notice is given and a hearing is held on a proposal to rezone a parcel of land from a low-density residential district to a high-density residential zoning district, is another hearing required if the city council decides to rezone the parcel to a medium-density residential district after hearing comments at the public hearing?

If the action taken is not substantially different from that originally proposed, no additional hearings are required. A change to a zoning proposal is not considered "substantially different" if the change is favorable to those who requested that change, if the action taken is of the same fundamental character as that proposed in the original public notice, and if the notice indicated that changes might be made after public comments are heard. As a general rule, amending the proposal to rezone less land or to allow a similar but less significant change in its uses will not require a new hearing. If a large area is proposed for rezoning and individual properties are shifted from one zoning district to another between the notice of the hearing and the hearing, a new notice and hearing is required even if the changes were made in response to landowner requests.

A hearing may be continued without advertising again if the board wants to allow additional comment at a future date. In these instances, the date, time, and place of the continuation of the hearing must be announced prior to closing the initial hearing.

If there are substantial changes in the zoning amendment to be considered, a new hearing is required. The additional hearing is subject to the same notice requirements as the initial hearing.

Planning Board Review

State law requires that all proposed zoning amendments be reviewed by the planning board (sometimes called the "planning commission" or "zoning commission") prior to action by the governing board. The planning board must be given up to thirty days for this review. The governing board can proceed with action on the proposed amendment whenever the planning board comment is received or at the end of the thirty-day review period if no written comment is received. The planning board comment must address whether the proposed amendment is consistent with the comprehensive plan and any other officially adopted plans that are applicable. The planning board can also address any other issues it deems appropriate.

There is no requirement for a positive recommendation from the planning board. Their recommendation is advisory only. Yet because the planning board often has detailed familiarity with the comprehensive plan and with neighborhood concerns and has given the proposal a thoughtful review, its recommendation is usually given considerable weight by the governing board.

There is no statutory requirement for a public hearing by the planning board before it makes a recommendation. Some zoning ordinances require a planning board hearing, some provide for a joint public hearing by the planning board and governing board, and some just provide that the planning board have a public meeting to discuss the proposal.

Decision Making
Factors to Consider

Primary factors to consider when making a zoning decision are generally the potential land use impacts on the landowner, the neighbors, and the public. Other factors, such as the suitability of the site for the proposed use, impacts on traffic, the environment, neighborhood character, utilities, schools, and the like, are also reasonable and appropriate to consider. Consistency with applicable plans and policies is also important, but the provisions in plans are not binding. Neither are past decisions; consideration of how similar proposals have been dealt with in the past can play a role, but each proposal must be examined on its own merits.

Factors that may not be a part of the decision on a rezoning or a text amendment include the ethnicity, religion, income, or "character" of residents subject to the proposal. Whether a project would be owner-occupied is not a legitimate zoning consideration. For example, allowing an accessory apartment in a single-family zoning district only if the principal dwelling or the apartment is owner-occupied is impermissible.

Protest Petitions

Neither the landowner nor the neighbors have any legal right to the continuation of any particular zoning on a piece of property. A decision on whether and how to rezone property is left to the discretion and good judgment of elected officials, the notion being that if the citizens do not approve of the officials' decisions, the remedy is at the ballot box. But in cities a further protection, the protest petition, provides a degree of additional stability to zoning, allowing citizens to have more say in a decision.

The protest petition was included in the original 1916 New York zoning ordinance and the model code that was adopted by most states, North Carolina included. The state statutes provide that if the owners of a sufficient amount of land most directly affected file such a petition, a municipal zoning amendment can be adopted only if approved by a three-fourths majority of the city council. The three-fourths majority is calculated on the basis of governing board members eligible to vote on the rezoning—vacant seats and the seats of members not eligible to vote due to a conflict of interest are not considered in making the calculation. This protest option must be provided by city governments, but the state statutes do not include a similar provision for counties.

There are two qualifying areas for a protest petition. The first requires a protest from the owners of 20 percent of the land included within the map amendment. The second requires a protest from the owners of 5 percent of the land included within a 100-foot wide buffer surrounding the property to be rezoned. A street right-of-way is not considered in computing this 100-foot buffer unless that right-of-way is more than 100 feet wide. These areas are illustrated in Figure 7.1. If more than one area is being considered in a rezoning proposal, separate protest petitions can be made for each discrete area.

The 20 percent and 5 percent requirements refer to the land area, not the number of owners. For example, if a single person owns 20 percent of the land proposed for rezoning, that individual can file a protest petition and trigger the three-fourths vote requirement. If only part of a parcel of land is proposed to be rezoned, the 100-foot buffer is measured from the property line, not from the zoning district boundary. Figure 7.2 illustrates this.

Certain procedural requirements must be met for the protest petition to be valid. The petition must be in writing, it must be signed by the owners of the property, and it must be filed at least two working days before the day of the advertised public hearing. For example, if the hearing is advertised for a Tuesday evening, the protest must be filed by the close of business on the previous Thursday (with Friday and Monday being the two working days prior to the day of the hearing). This allows the city sufficient time to calculate whether the protestors own a sufficient amount of a qualifying area. Cities may require the protest to be filed on a form provided by the city.

Protest petitions can be used only to object to changes in the zoning map. They cannot be filed to protest amendments to the zoning text. They cannot be filed to protest the initial zoning of an area, such as when zoning is first adopted for newly annexed territory of a city. Likewise, they cannot be used to protest modest changes in special and conditional use districts or conditional zoning amendments. A person may withdraw his or her signature to

Figure 7.1 Protest Areas

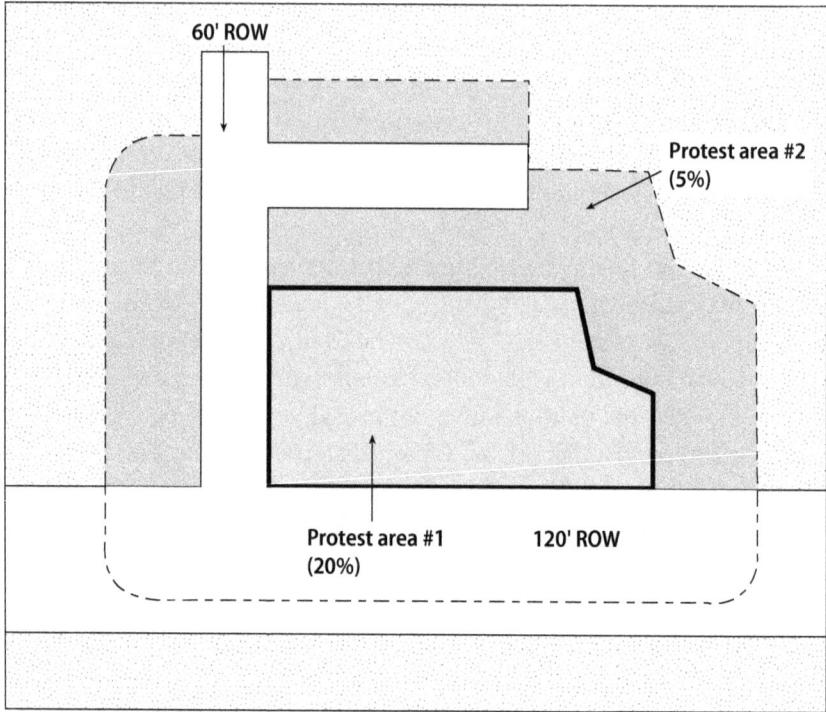

60' ROW

Protest area #2
(5%)

Protest area #1
(20%)

120' ROW

Protest petitions may be filed by the owners of 20 percent of the area being rezoned or 5 percent of the land within 100 feet of that area.

a protest petition at any time prior to the vote on the proposed amendment. The sufficiency of the protest is measured at the time of the vote.

While a valid protest petition can trigger a supermajority voting requirement, the general rule in North Carolina is that zoning decisions cannot be submitted to the voters. A small number of North Carolina jurisdictions, most notably Greensboro, have a procedure that allows a public referendum on a zoning change. The referendum is triggered by presentation of a petition of a sufficient number of qualified voters objecting to a rezoning. Special authorization by the General Assembly is necessary for zoning referenda. Absent such legislative authorization, a city or county cannot have a referendum on a zoning adoption, amendment, or repeal.

Figure 7.2   Measurement of Buffer Area

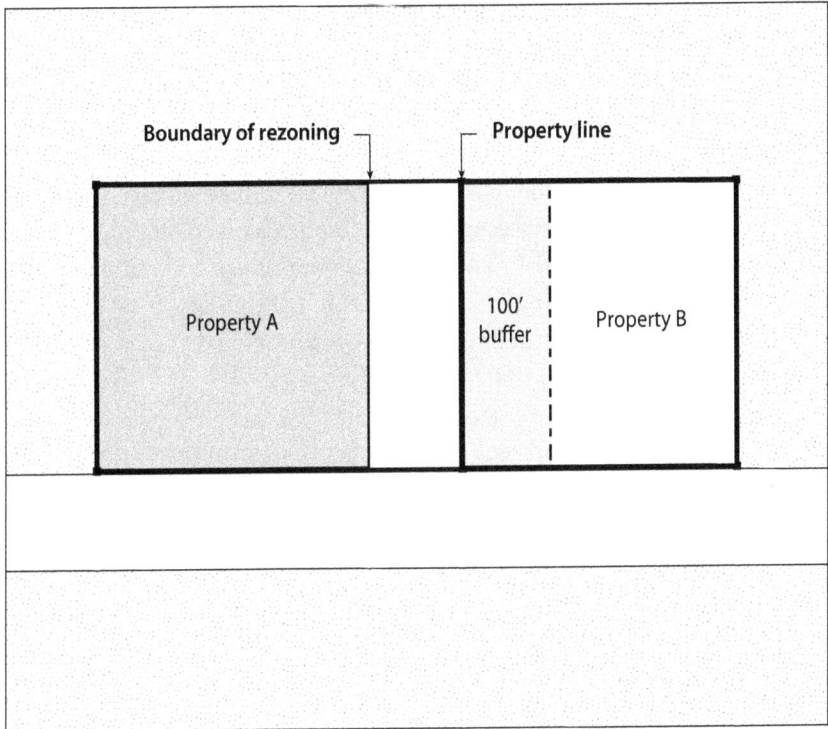

The 100-foot buffer is measured from the property line if less than an entire parcel is proposed for rezoning.

Conflicts of Interest

Members of city councils, boards of county commissioners, and planning boards must act in the public interest and not to advance their own financial interests. North Carolina has largely been spared scandals regarding bribery for rezonings. There are rarely even allegations that a local official has abused the development regulation power for personal gain. Still, the courts and legislature have recognized that these decisions can have substantial financial impacts—a simple rezoning can double or triple a property's value—and that public confidence in the integrity of the decision-making process is critical.

Therefore state law prohibits a member of an elected board or a planning board from voting on a zoning ordinance amendment where there is a potential financial conflict of interest. The statutes provide that if the outcome of the vote is "reasonably likely to have a direct, substantial, and readily identifiable financial impact"[1] on the member, the member must not vote on it. A speculative or minor financial impact is not disqualifying. Nor is a member disqualified from participating in the discussion if he or she has a conflict—only voting on the matter is prohibited.

In contrast to quasi-judicial decisions, impartiality is not required for legislative decisions. Decisions about ordinance adoption, amendment, or repeal require policy judgment by elected officials. These officials' personal knowledge, positions on issues important to citizens, and judgment about the preferred course for the community are important and valid components of the decision-making process. Expression of opinions, bias, and communication with citizens about the subject of a hearing do not disqualify a member from voting in legislative decisions.

While there is no requirement for impartiality in public policy choices, there are constitutional protections from bias based on race, ethnicity, or religion. For example, denying a rezoning for a place of worship based on which particular religion would be practiced there is impermissible. Also, a zoning decision based solely on personal animosity toward the applicant rather than any plausible public policy rationale would be unconstitutional.

The rule prohibiting financial conflicts of interest for legislative matters should be distinguished from the more strict rules on conflicts of interest in quasi-judicial matters (see Chapter 8 for more details). If a governing board or planning board makes special or conditional use permit decisions, for example, they must not participate in the discussion or voting if they have a personal bias, a predetermined opinion on the matter, a close family or business tie to a party, or a financial interest in the outcome.

Governing Board Statement

The decision to adopt, amend, or repeal a zoning ordinance is a legislative policy choice of the governing board. Formal findings of fact are not required, as is the case for all quasi-judicial decisions. However, the zoning statutes were amended in 2005 to require that city and county governing boards adopt a statement explaining the rationale for their decisions on zoning amendments.

Whenever the city council or board of county commissioners makes a decision to adopt or reject a zoning amendment, the board must approve a written statement describing whether the action is consistent with an adopted comprehensive plan. The board is not required to follow its adopted plans in zoning decisions, but it must carefully consider the plan and set out for public inspection its reasons for following the plan or not. The statement must also address why the board considers the action taken to be reasonable and in the public interest. The statement can be approved as part of the motion to adopt or reject the proposed amendment or it can be included in a separate resolution; the key factor is that the governing board itself must clearly indicate the board's position on the issue. While the substance of the statement is not subject to judicial review, failure to clearly approve a statement will lead to invalidation of the amendment if there is a judicial challenge.

Voting

In the absence of a valid protest petition to a zoning ordinance amendment, the normal rules for voting on an ordinance apply to adoption, amendment, or repeal of a development regulation.

For cities, state law requires that ordinances be adopted by a simple majority of all members of the council not excused from voting, except that a two-thirds vote is required to adopt an ordinance on the date the subject matter is first voted on by the council. For counties, the law requires a simple majority vote to adopt a land development regulation. If the statutes do not require a public hearing on a county ordinance, a unanimous vote of the county commissioners is required to adopt it at the first meeting it is taken up. However, since all proposed development ordinance adoptions and amendments require a public hearing, they are exempt from this unanimity on first reading provision.[2]

Corrections to Ordinance Errors

Occasionally an error will be discovered in the text of a development ordinance or on a zoning map. The process that must be used to fix the error depends on whether the mistake was made before or after adoption of the error.

If the error occurred after the governing board voted on the matter, the fix is easy and can be made immediately. If there was a clerical mistake—what the courts sometimes call a "scrivener's error"—in codifying the text or a rezoning, the staff can make an immediate correction so that the ordinance and map accurately reflect the true action taken by the city council or board of commissioners. Even though it is not legally necessary for the governing board to take action to fix this type of error, it should be reported to the board and the correction noted in the minutes (and particularly cautious local governments may want the board to adopt a resolution noting and approving the correction).

But what if the error was made prior to the governing board action? Say a rezoning petition or the staff report on a rezoning has incorrectly identified the boundaries of a proposed rezoning. If the governing board adopts the rezoning with that incorrect boundary, the ordinance then includes the mistake. The ordinance text or zoning map then accurately reflects what the governing board actually did rather than what they may have thought they did. When the error is included in the version that was actually adopted, a legislative rather than a clerical correction is required. The "fix" must go through the full amendment process for the governing board to adopt the correction.

Judicial Review

In North Carolina, the adoption, amendment, and repeal of development ordinances can be challenged in court only by persons who have a specific personal interest (called "standing") in the decision and whose legal interests are directly and adversely affected by the decision. A group (such as a neighborhood association) also has standing to challenge an action if its individual members have standing.

State statutes provide that a challenge to a zoning map amendment (a rezoning) must be filed within two months of the date of the decision. A challenge to a zoning text amendment must be filed within one year, measured from when a person first obtains standing to challenge the action. Any challenge to the procedures followed in adopting the amendment must be filed within three years of the challenged action. Once the challenge is filed, the court will examine the decision to determine if the governing board followed proper procedures or violated the legal rights of those affected. If, for example, there was inadequate public notice of the hearing, the court will void the action taken by the governing board and the zoning will revert to whatever it was before that decision.

As a general rule, the courts give legislative decisions a presumption of validity as to the substance of the decision—the court will not second-guess the policy decisions of elected officials. Only those decisions that are clearly unreasonable or abusive of discretion, those that violate constitutional protections, and those that were made using improper procedures will be set aside. The exception to this general rule of judicial deference to the judgment of governing boards comes in court review of spot zoning (discussed in more detail in Chapter 9). There, the local government has the burden of showing that its zoning is reasonable.

Notes

1. The city conflict-of-interest statute on legislative zoning decisions is Section 160A-381(d) of the North Carolina General Statutes (hereinafter G.S.) and the comparable county statute is G.S. 153A-340(g).

2. The city voting statute is G.S. 160A-75. The county voting statute is G.S. 153A-45.

Chapter 8

Process for Making
Quasi-Judicial Decisions

Decisions on variances, special use permits, and conditional use permits and appeals of administrative decisions made by an administrator require special handling. These decisions, along with a few others, involve determining the facts of the case and exercising some degree of judgment and discretion. They are called quasi-judicial decisions, and they are subject to rather demanding procedural rules set forth by the courts, including the requirement of a formal evidentiary hearing. These rules apply to all citizen boards making quasi-judicial decisions, whether it is the city council, board of county commissioners, planning board, or board of adjustment.

Basis for Rules

Quasi-judicial zoning decisions differ from legislative zoning decisions (such as a rezoning) in a fundamental manner—these decisions involve applying zoning policies rather than setting new policies. In quasi-judicial decisions, the board making the decision must act much like a court to apply the ordinance (the law) to a specific case.

This fundamental difference leads to a very different set of procedures that must be followed by the board. When new policies are being set, as with a rezoning, the law is designed to make sure there is wide public notice and opportunity to comment. On the other hand, when the policies already set out in the ordinance are being applied to an individual case, the legal requirements shift to a focus on securing a fair and impartial hearing on the merits of the case.

These differences in legal requirements for different types of zoning decisions often confuse citizen board members as well as citizens participating in hearings. In legislative zoning hearings, citizens can appear and say whatever is on their minds. Community opinions and attitudes are important, legitimate considerations. In evidentiary hearings for quasi-judicial zoning decisions, however, the purpose of the hearing is to gather legally acceptable evidence in order to establish sufficient facts to apply the ordinance. The fact that a hundred angry citizens appear expressing the opinion that the proposed special use permit would be the worst thing to ever happen to the town should have little, if any, bearing on the decision. The question before the board is whether the proposal meets the standards in the ordinance, not whether it is popular among the citizenry. Citizen boards must keep this difference clearly in mind.

Furthermore, it is very helpful if the purpose and limitations of the hearing are fully explained to those appearing at these hearings. A handout for the applicants and neighbors can explain the ground rules for evidentiary hearings and help avoid misunderstandings and legal errors in how these hearings are conducted.

A board making a quasi-judicial decision must do two things. First it must determine the facts of the case. In this task, the board acts much like a jury in a court proceeding. Second, it must apply the standards in the ordinance to those facts. In this task the board acts much like a judge in applying the law (in this case the standards in the zoning ordinance) to a given set of facts. The terminology used by the statutes and zoning ordinances sometimes leads to confusion about these two responsibilities. For example, the ordinance may provide that a special use permit shall be issued "upon the board finding that the project will not have a significant adverse effect on neighboring property values." Even though the ordinance uses the term "finding," this is really the standard that is to be applied. The board must be careful to both "find the facts"—what exactly are the impacts on neighboring property values and why—and to make a "finding"—a conclusion as to whether any adverse impacts are significant.

Most quasi-judicial zoning decisions are made by boards of adjustment. However, North Carolina law also allows these decisions to be made by the planning board or the governing board. They must not, however, be assigned to a single staff member because state statutes require the decision to be made by a board. The rules discussed here apply whenever a quasi-judicial zoning decision is involved, regardless of which citizen board makes the decision.

Evidentiary Hearings

Hearings on quasi-judicial land use regulatory matters must be conducted in a fair and impartial manner. While the formal rules of evidence that apply in court need not be rigorously followed, zoning and land use evidentiary hearings are serious proceedings that significantly affect the legal rights of the parties. In conducting these hearings, the following guidelines apply.

Hearing Notice and Organization

Since the purpose of these hearings is to gather the necessary evidence on which to base a decision rather than broadly solicit public comment, the broad public notice requirements of legislative decisions do not apply to these hearings. For example, there is no state mandate for newspaper publication of the hearing notice.

State law does establish a uniform process for providing mailed and posted notice of the hearing. A notice must be mailed to the person or entity making the application, appeal, or request for the hearing. This notice must also be mailed to the owner of the affected property (if he or she is not the applicant) and to the owners of all abutting properties. County tax listings may be used to determine the owners to receive these mailings. The notice must be deposited in the mail at least ten but not more than twenty-five days prior to the hearing. A notice of the hearing must also be posted in this same time period on the affected site or adjacent right-of-way.

Some ordinances impose additional notice requirements, such as mailing the notice to all owners within a specified distance from the property or publication in the newspaper. The local government must also comply with any such supplemental notice requirements set by the ordinance.

The state's open meetings law applies to boards making quasi-judicial decisions. This means that the regular meeting schedule must be filed with the city or county clerk, additional notice is required for special meetings, and all of the hearing and the board's deliberations must be conducted in open, public session. The board may not go into a closed session to discuss the case after receiving the evidence. A board can go into closed session for the narrow purpose of a privileged legal discussion with its attorney. But that discussion would be limited to legal advice and cannot include a deliberation of the case or a policy discussion.

Unlike a court proceeding, quasi-judicial hearings do not have formal plaintiffs and defendants. The person who initiates the action (an applicant for a special or conditional use permit, a person appealing the zoning officer's determination or requesting a variance) is a "party" to the proceeding and has legal rights that must be protected. A person who is directly affected by the decision (such as a neighbor whose property value would be affected) may also ask to participate in the hearing and can be considered a party.

Members of the general public are not "parties." A person who is interested in the matter but who does not have a personal stake in the outcome (such as a likely effect on his or her property value) may attend and observe the hearing, but they have no legal right to offer evidence, ask questions, or otherwise directly participate in the matter. Only the parties whose legal rights are directly affected are entitled to participate. As a practical matter, many presiding officers will allow a person who is not a party to present evidence, but care must be used to be sure it is relevant to the case.

The board's chair presides at an evidentiary hearing. The chair generally maintains an orderly process, calls on parties to present evidence, and moderates discussion among board members. He or she rules on any motions made and may consult with the board's attorney during the hearing for legal advice.

Board members are expected to know, understand, and follow the rules for quasi-judicial decisions. They should respectfully receive and consider the evidence presented. Board members may ask questions of witnesses to clarify and explore the facts presented. Board members are public officers and, as such, have limited exposure to personal liability as a result of board actions. Members can be held liable for intentional torts (such as assaulting someone during a hearing) and for willful misconduct (such as intentionally denying a permit that should have been issued because of a personal vendetta against the applicant). Good faith mistakes or errors in judgment do not expose members to personal liability.

The state bar has advised that representing a party at the evidentiary hearing in a quasi-judicial zoning matter—presenting evidence, cross-examining witnesses, advising as to the evidence needed—is the practice of law and should only be done by licensed attorneys. Parties are not required to have lawyers and are free to represent themselves. Most North Carolina jurisdictions report this is still the norm, particularly in less populous jurisdictions, as applicants and opponents are only occasionally represented by attorneys. It is also important to note that this restriction does not limit local government staff members, the applicant, an applicant's surveyor or engineer, or neighbors from appearing at the hearing as witnesses and presenting facts, documents, or other evidence regarding the matter.

If there is insufficient time to hear all of the evidence at a hearing, the board can continue the hearing. If the date, time, and location of the continued hearing are announced before the original hearing is adjourned, no additional notice of the continued hearing is required.

Complete records must be kept of the hearing. These should include detailed minutes noting the identity of witnesses and providing a complete summary of their testimony. Any exhibits presented should be retained by the board and become a part of the case file. An audio- or videotape of the hearing should be made, as any party can request that a tape of the hearing be included in the record if there is a judicial appeal. On occasion the parties may want a verbatim transcript of the entire hearing. Any party has a right to prepare a verbatim transcript (which generally requires that a court reporter be present at the hearing), but the cost of doing so is borne by the party requesting it.

Evidence Gathering

Boards conducting evidentiary hearings on zoning matters have the authority to issue subpoenas to compel testimony or production of evidence deemed necessary to determine the matter. Parties may request the subpoena be issued by the chair of the board hearing the matter. The board chair rules on subpoena requests and any objections to a subpoena that may be filed. The chair's rulings on subpoenas can be appealed to the full board.

The person requesting a variance or special/conditional use permit has the burden of producing sufficient evidence for the board to conclude the standards have been met. If insufficient evidence is presented, the application must be denied (or the board can continue the hearing to a later date to receive additional evidence). Once sufficient evidence is presented that the standards are met, the applicant is entitled to approval. If conflicting evidence is presented, the board must determine which facts it believes are correct.

There must be "substantial, competent, and material evidence"[1] to support each critical factual determination. Key points need to be substantiated

Does a City Council Really Have to Follow All These Zoning Rules?
The *Humble Oil* Case

Many towns set up zoning ordinances so that the city council makes final decisions on special use permits. Because these elected officials are the ones who adopted the ordinance and set the standards for special use permits in the first place, surely they do not have to go through all of the formalities of putting folks under oath, taking evidence, and making written findings when they rule on quasi-judicial matters such as special use permit applications, right? Wrong. As the town council in Chapel Hill found out, the courts require that *any* board making quasi-judicial permit decisions follow all of the rules for a fair evidentiary hearing.

In the fall of 1970, the Humble Oil Company obtained options on property at the far west end of Franklin Street in Chapel Hill, near the town's border with Carrboro. Part of the property was vacant, part had two small houses, and part was a used-car lot. The company proposed clearing the property and putting in an automobile service station. The town's appearance commission approved the project and the application for a special use permit then went to a joint hearing by the town council and the planning board.

Seven persons appeared and briefly spoke against the proposal, all in very general terms. The minister of a nearby church felt the gas station would be a traffic problem unless traffic lights were installed. Another speaker objected to removal of a tree. Several others expressed the opinion that there were already too many gas stations downtown. One speaker simply said she opposed the project.

Hearing these concerns, the town council decided on the spot not to refer the case to the planning board for a recommendation, and then unanimously voted to deny the

The car lot above was the site of the proposed gasoline station involved in the *Humble Oil* litigation. It remained a used-car lot for over twenty years after the landowners won their case.

permit on the basis of potential traffic problems. The company sued, contending its constitutional right to a fair hearing had been denied.

The North Carolina Supreme Court agreed with the applicant.[a] The court held that whenever a quasi-judicial zoning decision is made, the board making that decision must abide by all of the rules for a fair hearing—sworn testimony, cross-examination, adequate evidence in the record to support the decision, and written findings of fact. (State statutes have since recodified this requirement.) Since the only information on traffic hazards in the record was the lay opinion of a minister, the court ruled the town council had not complied with the standards for a fair hearing. The court sent the case back to the town for a new hearing and decision.

These pizza and oil change businesses were eventually built on the Humble Oil site.

So, did the Humble Oil Company then build its gas station? No. By the time the case was returned to the city in January 1974, a national gasoline shortage had emerged. Existing stations were only able to open a few days a week, so the applicant did not pursue the matter. The lot (see photo on the previous page) remained essentially unchanged for the next twenty years.

However, in 1995, the town issued a special use permit for a quick-oil-change business on a portion of the site, which was built and is now in use (see photo above). Thus an automobile service facility finally came to this spot in Chapel Hill some thirty years after the initial permit denial. This time the town's approval was conditioned on inclusion of additional street-oriented retail use (a pizza shop was included) in the project and a low brick wall to screen the parking. Traffic lights at both corners were installed long before the second application came along. The same minister was still serving the nearby church, but neither he nor others raised objections the second time around.

---

a. Humble Oil and Refining Co. v. Board of Aldermen, 284 N.C. 458 (1974).

by the factual evidence in the hearing record. The hearing record includes the application and attachments plus all of the testimony and exhibits submitted at the hearing. Conclusions about contested factual matters cannot be based on conjecture or assumptions. For example, for the board to find that neighboring property values would be significantly reduced by a proposed project, there must be evidence in the record to support that finding, such as testimony from a qualified real estate agent or appraiser about the impacts of a similar project elsewhere in town or presentation of facts that would allow a reasonable person to conclude property values would go down.

The application and any correspondence submitted as part of the application file is to be entered into the hearing record and should be considered by the board. Most application forms are designed to elicit information sufficient for a decision. Usually a staff member appears as the initial witness and presents the application file as an exhibit for the hearing record, thus establishing the factual foundation for the rest of the hearing. Someone familiar with the information in the application (usually the applicant or an agent of the applicant) should be available to answer any questions the board may have about the written submissions.

Those offering testimony are put under oath. This reminds witnesses of the seriousness of the matter and the necessity of presenting factual information, not opinions or speculation. All of the witnesses may be sworn in at one time at the beginning of the hearing or each witness may be sworn in as he or she begins to testify. While oaths may be waived if all of the parties agree, many local governments routinely swear in all witnesses, including the staff members and attorneys who are making presentations. If a witness has religious objections to taking an oath, he or she may affirm rather than swear an oath. The oath is generally administered by the chair of the board receiving the testimony (it may also be administered by the city or county clerk, the clerk to the board holding the hearing, or by any notary public). Testifying falsely under oath is a criminal offense.

The board may accept evidence if no objections are raised to it at the hearing or the board deems the evidence sufficiently trustworthy and reasonably reliable. Where conflicting evidence is presented, the board has the responsibility of deciding how much weight to accord each piece of evidence.

Parties have the right to cross-examine witnesses. The board can establish reasonable procedures for this, such as allowing questions to be posed only by a single representative of a party. Board members are also free to pose questions to anyone presenting evidence. Members of the public who are attending the hearing but who are not parties do not have the right to ask questions of witnesses.

If a statement is being used as evidence to establish a fact, the person making that statement should be present at the hearing to testify and be subject to cross-examination. If a statement from a person who is not present is offered and it is the best evidence available, it can be received by the board if there is no objection to its introduction and the board deems it sufficiently trustworthy. But the board may well decide to limit the weight or credibility it gives such evidence, and critical findings of fact should not be based on hearsay.

The board may accept and rely on letters about the project received from other government agencies (provided these letters are entered as exhibits in the record). Some boards that make quasi-judicial decisions receive recommendations from an advisory board (such as the planning board making a recommendation on a special use permit). While the board may consider the recommendation, it is not factual evidence; to be considered in the decision, any factual information presented to the advisory board would also have to be presented at the hearing held by the deciding board.

If the hearing is an appeal of an officer's determination, state law requires the officer to be present as a witness at the hearing.

Boards need facts for their findings, not opinions. Opinion evidence (unless offered by a properly qualified expert witness) is generally not allowed and cannot be the basis for critical findings. The courts have frequently invalidated decisions based upon "speculative opinions and generalized fears" expressed in lay witness testimony. In this regard evidentiary and legislative hearings differ considerably. In a legislative hearing, such as on a proposed rezoning, speakers are free to offer their unvarnished opinions, but this is not true for evidentiary hearings. Section 160A-393(k) of the North Carolina General Statutes (hereinafter G.S.) specifically prohibits use of opinion testimony from nonexpert witnesses on

1. the proposed project's impact on property values,
2. the safety impacts of vehicular traffic expected to be generated by a proposed project, and
3. matters in which only expert testimony would be admissible in court.

A witness offering an opinion, even if an expert, must present the factual information and analysis that is the foundation of the offered opinion.

Persons affected by a decision have the legal right to hear all of the information presented to board members and to know all of the facts being considered by the board. Therefore members of the decision-making body are not allowed to discuss the case or gather evidence outside of the hearing (what the courts term ex parte communication). Only facts presented to the full board at the hearing may be considered.

It is permissible for board members to view the site in question before the hearing. A member who has made a site visit or who is otherwise familiar with the site should note that at the hearing and mention any observations that are important to the decision or that are not otherwise noted in the hearing record.

It is not appropriate for a board member to discuss a pending case with the applicant, neighbors, or the local government staff. If a member has questions of these people, he or she should ask them at the hearing.

If a member has special knowledge about a site or case, the member should disclose that at the hearing. A member who fails to disclose any ex parte communications is prohibited from participating in the case.

Once a hearing is closed, new testimony or evidence may not be added to the record. For this reason, many local governments do not "close" the hearing until all deliberation is concluded and the board is ready to vote. For example, the board may conclude receipt of testimony and move into deliberation but then want to ask a clarifying question of the staff or a party; this is permissible if the hearing has not been closed. If the hearing has been closed and the board continues to meet to deliberate, adopt findings, and vote, no additional evidence may be received.

While unduly repetitious or irrelevant testimony can be barred, an arbitrary time limit on the hearing should not be used. It would not be appropriate, for example, to limit each side in a variance proceeding to five minutes to present their case. It is acceptable to allow only a single witness representing a group with similar concerns.

Witnesses may present documents, photos, maps, or other exhibits. Once presented for consideration by the board, exhibits are evidence in the hearing (and must be retained by the board). Each exhibit should be clearly labeled and numbered as it is received into evidence and kept in the files as part of the hearing record.

Decision Making

If an individual board member has a strong personal interest in a case, he or she must not participate in that case. "Personal interest" includes a financial interest in the outcome; a close personal, family, or business relation with the parties; a predetermined opinion about the outcome (a disqualifying bias); or undisclosed outside communications about the case. Having some opinions about the matter does not disqualify a member, but if those opinions rise to the level of a fixed opinion that is not susceptible to change ("My mind is made up. Don't confuse me with the facts."), then the member must be disqualified. This constitutional and statutory right to an impartial decision-maker applies to all boards making quasi-judicial decisions, even elected officials.

The usual practice is for the member with a disqualifying conflict to state that he or she has a conflict and will not be participating (state statutes require a governing board to vote to excuse a member with a conflict). If an objection to a member's participation is raised and the member does not step aside, the remaining members of the board by majority vote decide if that member can participate. Whenever a member is disqualified, that member must not participate in the hearing in any way, neither asking questions, nor debating, nor voting on the case. It is a good practice, though not legally required, for a member with a conflict of interest to physically leave the room while that case is being handled by the board.

Determining when a person has an impermissible bias in these cases can be difficult. If, for example, a member boldly announces his or her intended vote on a special use permit application prior to hearing the evidence, that member clearly has a fixed opinion and must not participate in the case. On the other hand, simply knowing some of the parties or having expressed an opinion about the general policies involved with a case is generally not impermissible bias if the member can fairly state he or she will make a decision based on the evidence presented and ordinance standards. But exactly where the line is between impermissible bias and permissible general opinions that do not affect a vote is often unclear. The statute on review of quasi-judicial zoning decisions recognizes the complications in determining whether bias exists, as G.S. 160A-393(j) allows the hearing record on review to be supplemented with affidavits, testimony, or documents to determine if members of the decision-making board were sufficiently impartial.

A member who was not present for all of the hearings may still vote on the matter, but only if such a vote is not prohibited by the local ordinance or rules of procedure and only if the member has full access to all of the evidence (copies of the minutes of the hearing are sufficient) presented at any portion of the hearing the member missed.

State statutes impose a special voting requirement for some quasi-judicial decisions. A four-fifths vote rather than a simple majority is required in order for a zoning board of adjustment to grant a variance. A "four-fifths vote" means four-fifths of the entire board must vote in favor of the proposal, not just four-fifths of those present and voting. In the case of a ten-member board of adjustment with two members absent, a unanimous, eight-to-zero vote would be necessary (eight being four-fifths of the entire ten-member board). Vacant seats and the seats of a member who is disqualified from voting due to a conflict of interest (if there is no qualified alternate member available to take that seat) are not considered in making the four-fifths calculation. This supermajority requirement is an additional reason that most boards of adjustment have alternate members who can take an absent or disqualified member's place.

The board must render its decision in writing. This is necessary to let the parties—and, if the matter is appealed, the courts—know what the board concluded about the facts of the case. A simple written conclusion that the standards were or were not met is not sufficient, nor is a letter just stating that the permit has been issued or denied. The written decision needs to provide enough detail to let the reader know how the board determined any contested facts. Proposed factual findings can be drafted ahead of time (by the applicant, the opponents, or the staff) and adopted at the meeting, or findings can be composed at the conclusion of the hearing. Whether the written decision takes the form of a letter from the board chair or a more formal order setting out findings of fact and conclusions of law, the decision document must clearly set out the board's determination of contested facts and the decision made.

The written decision must be signed by the chair (or other duly authorized member) of the decision-making board. The decision is effective when it is filed with the clerk to the board. The decision must be delivered to the applicant, to the property owner (if the property owner was not the applicant), and to anyone who has made a written request for a copy prior to the effective date of the decision. Delivery of the written decision can be made by personal delivery, email, or first-class mail. The time period for appeals to court only starts to run when the written decision is both delivered and filed.

The question of how to adopt findings when a minority of the board prevails requires particular attention. For example, if a five-member board of adjustment votes three to two to grant a variance, the variance is denied because it did not receive the required four-fifths majority. The minutes and written decision need to clearly set forth why the two dissenters voted as they did, but there is no requirement that a majority of the board agrees with or officially adopts those views.

Prior decisions are not legally binding on a board. Each case must be decided on its own individual merits. Subtle differences in individual facts and situations can lead to differing results. However, a board should be aware of previous decisions and, as a general rule, similar cases should usually produce similar results. If a board reaches a different result for a very similar fact situation, the board's written decision should clearly explain why there was a different conclusion.

Once a final decision is reached on a quasi-judicial zoning decision, the same matter cannot be brought back to the board for a rehearing. Unless there is a different application or conditions have changed on the site or in the ordinance, a board does not have the legal authority to rehear these cases. This is unlike a legislative rezoning decision where the same petition can be reconsidered after a waiting period set by the ordinance.

Judicial Review

Appeals of quasi-judicial decisions go directly to court. An applicant may not appeal a board of adjustment's quasi-judicial decision to the governing board or vice versa. Once a final binding decision has been rendered on any of these quasi-judicial zoning decisions, a person who is directly affected by the decision can appeal that decision to superior court in the county where the decision was made.

In order to have standing to bring a suit challenging a quasi-judicial decision, a party must have potentially suffered damages beyond those that would be suffered by the general public—the party must make a credible allegation that the action would harm the value or use and enjoyment of his or her property. In addition to reductions in property value, these "special damages" include harmful impacts from noise, light, traffic, stormwater runoff, and the like.

An appeal of a quasi-judicial decision to the court must be filed within thirty days of the effective date of the decision or its delivery to those entitled to get notice of the decision, whichever is later. However, a party in an enforcement action may challenge the validity of the ordinance whenever the enforcement action is initiated (provided there is a three-year maximum to raise procedural irregularities regarding the adoption of the ordinance or amendment). Appeals of other land use regulatory decisions, such as a subdivision plat approval or denial, are not subject to this thirty-day time limit, but they must still be filed within a reasonable time.

The superior court does not conduct a new hearing to determine the facts. Rather, it sits as an appeals court and bases its decision on the factual record established at the evidentiary hearing conducted by the local citizen board. The record includes all documents and exhibits submitted at the hearing and the minutes or transcript of the hearing. Supplemental evidence is limited to information needed to show standing, conflicts of interest, or constitutional matters beyond the scope of issues the board could address. This is one of the reasons it is important that adequate evidence be presented at the board hearing and that good records are kept of those proceedings. Probably the most frequent reason a citizen board's quasi-judicial zoning decision is overruled by the courts is that there was inadequate evidence in the record to support the board's findings of fact. If a board's findings of fact are supported by the record, the reviewing court is bound by those factual determinations.

Other factors considered by the courts when they review quasi-judicial decisions are whether proper procedures were followed in the decision-making process, whether there were errors made in interpreting the law, and whether the decision was "arbitrary and capricious." On this latter point, the court may not substitute its judgment for that of the citizen board; it does not second-guess a close call or consider whether the citizen board made the "right" decision. But if there is no rational basis for the decision, the court can overturn it.

Note

1. Section 160A-388(e2) of the North Carolina General Statutes. This statute codifies the standard on required evidence to support a quasi-judicial decision first set forth in *Humble Oil and Refining Co. v. Board of Aldermen*, 284 N.C. 458 (1974).

Chapter 9

Spot, Contract, and Conditional Zoning

When a local government rezones a relatively small area of land, special care must be taken to protect the rights of the landowner, the neighbors, and the community at large. These rezonings are sometimes referred to as "small scale rezonings." Courts give special scrutiny to spot zoning and potential contract zoning cases. There are legally permissible ways for local governments to craft zoning restrictions that are fitted to individual situations, principally through the use of conditional zoning. Conditional zoning, because of the potential for abuse, has special statutory limits, making it a legally complicated tool that should only be applied with great care.

Spot Zoning

Zoning is an exercise of governmental power for the overall public good. The courts generally defer to the judgment of elected officials as to just what this overall public good is. But when the zoning power is applied to a small area in a way that is different from the way it is applied to the surrounding area, particularly if the small area is owned by a single entity, the overall public good may not be served. Treating one parcel differently from the surrounding property raises concerns that the zoning may unfairly benefit or harm that owner (or the neighbors) or that improper factors—such as favoritism or antagonism toward an individual—may have motivated that zoning decision. If such a zoning action, called spot zoning, is challenged in court, the

Is There a Legal Way to Do Spot Zoning or Contract Zoning? The *Chrismon* Case

Serious disputes between neighbors about adjacent land uses frequently end up as zoning battles. Not only do such battles resolve individual disputes, they often shape the law on how zoning tools must be applied by all cities and counties. A Guilford County dispute between a homeowner seeking peace and quiet in the country and a business owner who needed to expand illustrates this.

Bruce Clapp owned and ran a small operation for drying grain adjacent to his home in rural Guilford County, a business begun in 1948. In 1969 he sold a portion of his property to Mr. and Mrs. William Chrismon for a residence. In 1980 Clapp expanded his grain drying operation to a portion of his property immediately behind the Chrismons' house and expanded the business (see the photo below) to include the sale of farm chemicals. The Chrismons were not happy about this and complained to the county. It turned out the entire site was zoned for agricultural and residential uses, so the county told Clapp he could not expand the business. Now Clapp was unhappy. So he promptly asked that the 5-acre portion of his land needed for the business expansion be rezoned to allow his business. The county commissioners sided with Clapp and rezoned the property to a district that allowed the operation if he got a conditional use permit—and they concurrently issued a conditional use permit. The county was then sued by the Chrismons, who alleged that this was illegal spot zoning and illegal contract zoning.

Property immediately behind the Chrismons' home was rezoned to allow this grain drying operation.

In a key zoning case,[a] the North Carolina Supreme Court upheld the county action. The court said this was indeed spot zoning, but it was not illegal because it was reasonable in this situation. The court found that this particular business was compatible with and beneficial to the surrounding farm community and that it was not a substantial departure from the uses already present in the neighborhood. The court also allowed the practice of creating a zoning district with only conditional uses (and no automatically approved permitted uses) and allowed the county commissioners to decide on the conditional use permit at the same time that the rezoning decision was made. This tool, conditional use district zoning, was subsequently adopted by many North Carolina cities and counties as a way of avoiding illegal contract zoning. The zoning statutes were subsequently amended to explicitly authorize conditional use districts (and were still later further amended to authorize purely legislative conditional zoning).

---

a. Chrismon v. Guilford Cnty., 322 N.C. 611 (1988).

court will not presume the zoning to be valid, but rather will review the zoning very carefully to ensure that it is reasonable and in the public interest. Courts apply this heightened spot zoning scrutiny to challenges of the initial zoning of a parcel or to a rezoning.

Just how small the area has to be to raise the spot zoning issue depends on the setting. In the center of a city with many zoning districts, a 5-acre rezoning may represent a relatively large zoning district and not be considered spot zoning. On the other hand, in a rural area where thousands of surrounding acres are zoned one way, a 50-acre rezoning may be spot zoning. In North Carolina the courts have invalidated spot zonings as small as one lot and as large as 50 acres.

In some states spot zoning is always illegal. North Carolina law permits spot zoning, but only if a local government can establish that a particular spot zoning is reasonable. Some states treat spot zoning as a quasi-judicial decision, reasoning that, for all practical purposes, it is more similar to a decision on an individual special or conditional use permit than to a legislative decision. The North Carolina courts have not taken that step, so neither evidentiary hearings nor formal findings are required. When spot zonings are challenged, however, the courts analyze the following factors on a case-by-case basis to determine if a particular spot zoning is reasonable. Thus cities and counties should ensure that the governing board considers and discusses these specific factors prior to adopting any spot zoning.

1. *The size and nature of the tract.* The larger the area of spot zoning the more likely it is to be reasonable. Singling out an individual lot for special zoning treatment is more suspect than creating a zoning district that involves multiple parcels and owners. Special site characteristics, such as topography, availability of utilities, or access to rail or highways, can be important in this analysis.

2. *Compatibility with existing plans.* If a clear public policy rationale for the different zoning treatment is set out in the local government's adopted plans, that evidences a public purpose for the zoning. By contrast, a zoning action that is inconsistent with a plan may indicate special treatment that is contrary to the public interest and thus be unreasonable.

3. *The impact of the zoning decision on the landowner, the immediate neighbors, and the surrounding community.* An action that is of great benefit to the owner and only a mild inconvenience for the

neighbors may be reasonable, while a zoning decision that significantly harms the neighbors while only modestly benefiting the owner would be unreasonable.

4. *The relationship between the newly allowed uses in a spot rezoning and the previously allowed uses.* The degree of difference in the existing surrounding land uses and the proposed new use is also important. The greater the difference in allowed uses, the more likely the rezoning will be found unreasonable. For example, in an area previously zoned for residential uses, allowing slightly higher residential density may be reasonable while allowing industrial uses would be unreasonable.

The key question in a court's review of an alleged illegal spot zoning is whether the zoning power is being exercised in the public interest rather than for the benefit of a few owners at the expense of the community. Sometimes very small zoning districts are justified and reasonable.

State statutes now require that a statement analyzing the reasonabless of the proposed rezoning be prepared for each petition for a small-scale rezoning (including every petition for the conditional rezoning or conditional use district rezoning discussed below). That statement should carefully address each of the mandatory factors listed above, as it may serve as the foundation of showing why the action taken was not illegal spot zoning.

Contract Zoning

In contract zoning, the government and a landowner enter into a private agreement as to how the zoning power will be exercised. For example, a local government might agree to rezone a parcel of land from a residential to a commercial zoning district in return for the owner's promise to build a new swimming pool for the city's park system.

Tempting though it may be to use them, contract zoning and similar agreements are illegal in North Carolina. The zoning power must be exercised for the public good, not used as a bargaining chip in ad hoc negotiations with individual landowners. Therefore a city or county must avoid any quid pro quo agreement in a rezoning. It is possible to have conditions on a rezoning that establish obligations on the part of the landowner, but only in the context of conditional zoning, as discussed below.

Though not technically contract zoning, the following kind of agreement is also illegal in North Carolina: a landowner requests a rezoning to accommodate a specific project and the city or county governing board considers only that project rather than the full range of uses that would be allowed in the new zoning district. If an owner promises the governing board that the new zoning would be used only for a particular project, that promise is not binding. Once the property is rezoned, the owner (and anyone the person may sell the property to) can undertake any use permitted in the new zoning district.

If it is clear that the governing board did not consider the full range of uses allowed in the new zoning district, the courts will invalidate the rezoning. For these reasons, many local governments forbid someone proposing a rezoning to a conventional zoning district from even mentioning what specific use is planned for the site.

It is not, however, illegal for a rezoning to be made to accommodate a specific use or project. The governing board can even discuss that project. However, if a specific use is mentioned, the record should clearly show that the governing board was aware of the full range of uses that would be allowed in the new district and that the governing board concluded that any of those permitted uses (not just the specific project proposed) would be suitable. Thus where a particular project has been discussed, the staff will typically read into the record all of the potential uses that would be permitted by the rezoning and will note that any of these uses would be authorized, not just that particular project.

Special conditions on a conventional rezoning—such as requiring a buffer strip of a certain size—are not enforceable. Only those standards that apply to all property in the zoning district are legally enforceable. In this situation, the North Carolina courts will generally uphold the rezoning but without the invalid condition. The only way to apply individualized conditions with a rezoning is through use of the conditional zoning tools discussed below.

Conditional Zoning

Conditional zoning is increasingly used in North Carolina to avoid legal problems with contract zoning. This tool allows the local government to legally discuss a particular project with an owner and the neighbors before rezoning a property, but only if the proper procedures are followed precisely. Conditional zoning is legal in North Carolina if it is correctly applied. There are two ways to do this—conditional use district zoning and conditional zoning. North Carolina cities and counties are authorized to use either or both of these tools. The first of these tools—conditional use district rezoning—originated in this state in the 1980s, with conditional zoning coming into use several years later.

A *conditional use district rezoning* is initiated when the owner asks for a rezoning to a new zoning district that does not have any automatically permitted uses, only uses allowed by the issuance of a special or conditional use permit. In the usual conditional use district rezoning process, the owner applies for a special or conditional use permit for a particular project at the same time the rezoning is requested. The two decisions (the rezoning and the permit) are considered in a single proceeding.

Conditional use district zoning is a complicated process. Although the rezoning request and the permit application are processed at the same time, the governing board treats the two proposals as legally independent, separate decisions. All of the detailed conditions and specific restrictions on the project are attached to the conditional or special use permit (which is legal) rather than to the rezoning itself (which would not be enforceable). In order to do this the board must make two decisions that have very different procedural requirements, but the common practice has been to make both decisions at the same time and with a single hearing. As a practical matter, this means that while all of the notice, planning board referrals, and other procedures for a legislative decision (see Chapter 7) must be observed, the more demanding requirements of an evidentiary hearing for quasi-judicial matters, such as not discussing the case with proponents or opponents outside of the formal hearing (see Chapter 8), must also be observed. These requirements create a demanding and complicated hearing and decision-making process.

An alternative that has been approved by both the courts and the legislature is purely legislative *conditional zoning*. This is different from a conditional use district in that there is no accompanying special or conditional use permit. All of the site-specific standards and conditions (often including a site plan) are incorporated into the zoning district regulations. Conditional zoning is proving to be very popular with elected officials, landowners, and many neighbors because it allows zoning to be tailored more carefully to a particular situation without having the strictures of a quasi-judicial decision. In some of the state's larger cities, 80 to 90 percent of the rezonings are conditional zoning rather than rezonings to a conventional zoning district without individualized conditions.

This negotiated approach to a legislative decision allows maximum flexibility to tailor regulations to a particular site and project. But it also has great potential for abuse—both in terms of impacts on individual landowners seeking approval and their neighbors and on the public interests zoning is supposed to promote. Thus special restrictions have been placed on conditional zoning. State law only allows implementation of conditional zoning and conditional use districts at the owner's request. They cannot be imposed without the owner's agreement. The individual conditions and site-specific standards that can be imposed are limited to those that are needed to bring a project into compliance with city and county ordinances and adopted plans and to those addressing the impacts reasonably expected to be generated by use of the site. Conditional zoning is not exempt from a spot zoning challenge. If the new district is relatively small—and virtually all of these are—the local government must assure that all of the factors defining reasonable spot zoning are fully considered and that the public hearing record reflects that consideration.

Conditional zoning provides important opportunities to carefully tailor regulations to address the interests of the landowner, the neighbors, and the public. A governing board will use conditional zoning when it concludes that a particular project should be approved but that the standards in the comparable conventional zoning district are insufficient to protect neighbors or public interests (perhaps because the conventional zoning allows other uses not suitable for the site or dimensional standards inadequate to preserve the neighborhood). Conditional zoning often allows a developer to proceed with a project in a way that addresses site-specific concerns of neighbors and the local government, while a rezoning to a conventional district would not have been adopted.

Conditional use districts and conditional zoning are complicated and must be carefully applied. A good land use plan is vital to frame appropriate conditions within a particular context, avoiding "ad hocery run amuck," as some critics have described widespread use of conditional zoning. When employed with thoughtfulness and deliberation, these are increasingly important and useful zoning tools.

Chapter 10

Special and Conditional Use Permits

Early zoning ordinances set out a list of land uses permitted in each zoning district, with all other uses prohibited in that district. Determining whether a particular use was allowed was a simple yes or no proposition. For example, an apartment building could be a permitted use in an R-10 district, in which case it is automatically allowed (sometimes referred to as a "use by right"). Otherwise it was prohibited.

In the 1960s many local governments decided additional zoning flexibility was desirable—that in addition to yes or no, sometimes the initial answer should be maybe. Perhaps an apartment building is an acceptable use in an R-10 district, but only under certain circumstances. Special and conditional use permits were added to zoning ordinances to provide this flexibility. Specific authority to use special and conditional use permits was added to the North Carolina zoning statutes in 1967.

Most modern zoning ordinances set up a category for these "maybes" of the zoning world. These may be called a special use permit, a conditional use permit, or a special exception (the terms are legally the same and are interchangeable).[1] They are uses that are not automatically permitted in a particular zoning district but are permitted if certain specified conditions are met. Decisions on these permits are quasi-judicial, so all of the hearing requirements discussed in Chapter 8 apply to how cities and counties deal with these applications.

Decision-Making Body

The decisions on permit applications may be made by the governing board, the board of adjustment, or the planning board. These decisions are not allocated on an ad hoc basis—each local government specifies the decision-making body in its zoning ordinance. These decisions cannot be assigned to an individual staff member.

It is possible to assign some of these decisions to one board and some to a different board. Often, if a zoning ordinance splits the decisions on such permits between two boards, to reduce confusion each board will use a different name for the permit it grants. For example, the permits granted by the governing board may be called "special use permits" and those granted by the board of adjustment "conditional use permits." Even so, both are quasi-judicial decisions, both require a full evidentiary hearing, and all of the standards discussed in Chapter 8 apply no matter which board is making the decision.

A number of cities and counties provide for an advisory review of special and conditional use permits by the planning board, perhaps using the required planning board review of rezonings as a model. While this is legally permissible, care must be taken to assure that any evidence to be considered by the decision-making board is properly presented to that board. If the governing board makes the final decision and holds the formal evidentiary hearing on the permit application, only evidence presented at that hearing may be considered. Evidence that is presented only to the advisory board cannot be the basis for a decision.

Standards for Decision

The zoning ordinance itself must spell out the standards used to determine special and conditional use permits. An ordinance could specify, for example, that duplexes, normally not allowed in a single-family residential district, are permissible with a special use permit anywhere in that district, but only upon a determination that (1) they are located on a lot that contains at least 20,000 square feet, (2) there is sufficient road frontage for two driveways at least 50 feet apart, and (3) the proposed unit's appearance is compatible with the surrounding houses.

The decision-making standards must be included in the text of the ordinance. They cannot be developed on a case-by-case basis, as that would be leaving these decisions to the unfettered discretion of the board making the decision. This is not permissible, even if it is the city council or board of county commissioners making the decision. The decision to grant or deny the permit, or to impose conditions on an approval, must be based on the standards that are actually in the ordinance and that are clearly indicated as the standards to be applied to this decision.

The standards must provide sufficient guidance for decision. The applicant and neighbors, the board making the decision, and a court reviewing the decision all need to know what the ordinance requires for approval. The courts have held there is inadequate guidance if the ordinance only provides an extremely general standard, such as that the project be in the public interest or that it be consistent with the purposes of the ordinance.

The courts have approved use of a set of five relatively general standards that are now incorporated into most North Carolina zoning ordinances. They are that the project:

1. not materially endanger the public health and safety,
2. meet all required conditions and specifications,
3. not substantially injure the value of adjoining property (or, alternatively, that it be a public necessity),
4. be in harmony with the surrounding area and compatible with the surrounding neighborhood, and
5. be in general conformance with adopted plans.

One of the most difficult of these general standards to apply is a determination of whether a proposed project is harmonious or compatible with the surrounding neighborhood. The courts have said it is appropriate to consider the types of uses involved; the density or intensity of the development; and the size, location, style, and appearance of the buildings and open space. However, if an ordinance authorizes a special or conditional use in a particular zoning district, presumably that use is harmonious with the neighborhood, provided the specified conditions are met. Those opposing the permit must provide evidence that the particular project design or site conditions produce the incompatibility, not the use in and of itself.

In addition to these general standards, some cities and counties also include specific standards for particular types of special uses. Typical specific standards include minimum lot sizes, buffering or landscaping requirements, special setbacks, and the like. Ordinances can use a combination of general and specific standards. For example, all special and conditional uses may be required to meet four or five general standards and then the ordinance sets out a list of additional specific standards for various individual uses.

The statutes do not explicitly address amendment or revocation of special and conditional use permits. Many ordinances allow staff approval of minor modifications to these permits, but the ordinance should specifically authorize these modifications and define what is "minor." Any substantial change should be subject to the same application and hearing procedures used with the initial approval of these permits. If there is a violation of the terms of the permit, it likely can be revoked, but the decision to revoke is probably quasi-judicial. Therefore the same notice and hearing requirements used for initially issuing the permit should be followed in consideration of revocation. Some ordinances also provide that a permittee may voluntarily relinquish a special or conditional use permit. This relinquishment should be in writing and maintained in the local government files.

Once issued, a special or conditional use permit can be transferred by the applicant to another person, but not to another property. The permit applies to the property involved, not to the person receiving it.

Evidence Required

The burden is on the applicant to present sufficient evidence to allow the board to make a finding that the required standards will be met. The burden is on an opponent to the permit to present evidence that a general standard will not be met.

If insufficient evidence is presented that the required standards will be met, the permit must be denied. If uncontradicted evidence is presented that all of the standards will be met, the board must issue the permit. Similarly, if uncontradicted evidence is presented that one of the general or specific standards will not be met, the permit must be denied. If there is conflicting evidence, the board decides what the facts are and issues or denies the permit accordingly. When there are contested facts, the written decision of the board must clearly indicate what the board's determination of those facts are.

Conditions

The board can impose additional unique, project-specific conditions on special and conditional use permits. The ordinance should explicitly provide authority to impose conditions and address the process to be followed in doing so.

It is very important to note that the board does not have the authority to impose any conditions it wants. Each condition must be related to the standards in the ordinance. There must be substantial evidence in the record to justify the imposition of any conditions. Conditions that impose an exaction must be reasonably related and proportionate to the anticipated impacts of the permitted project (see Chapter 15 for the constitutional limits on exactions). The ordinance can place an expiration date on a special use permit as well, so that if a building permit for the project is not secured within a certain time, the permit expires.

When ownership of the property subject to a special or conditional use permit changes, all of the conditions included in the original permit still apply to the new owner. For this reason, some local governments require that special use permits be recorded in the chain of title so that future purchasers of a property will be fully aware of all permit conditions.

Note

1. For further information on special and conditional use permits, see DAVID W. OWENS, SPECIAL USE PERMITS IN NORTH CAROLINA ZONING (Special Series No. 22, Apr. 2007).

Chapter 11

Variances

From their inception, zoning ordinances must have included a mechanism to allow landowners to seek relief from the strict application of the ordinance short of going to court. Under specified circumstances, a landowner may be granted permission to develop in a manner contrary to the rules that otherwise apply to everyone in the jurisdiction. The legal authorization for certain exceptions to the rules—called variances—is required for zoning ordinances and may be allowed in other local development regulations. Even if the variance option is not expressly mentioned in an individual ordinance, state law requires that it be available to all landowners regulated by zoning (provided, of course, that the standards for approving a variance are met).

Variances are quasi-judicial decisions and must follow all of the procedural standards set out in Chapter 8, including a full evidentiary hearing on each case. Decision making on variances is usually assigned to the board of adjustment, though the ordinance can assign this function to the planning board or governing board.

The Variance Power

One of the most powerful zoning tools, and one of the most difficult to apply, is the variance. The applicant for a variance comes to the city or county with a proposal along these lines: "My project is inconsistent with your zoning requirements. However, what I want to do is consistent with what you are trying to accomplish with the ordinance and would have been allowed had this been considered when the ordinance was adopted. Furthermore, if I have to comply with the strict terms of the ordinance, not only will it not benefit the public, it will work a very real and serious hardship on me. Because of these peculiar circumstances, you are justified in granting me permission to do something contrary to the requirements of the zoning ordinance."

Since zoning ordinances were first drafted in the 1920s, the variance has been available as a safety valve for these situations. The underlying notion of the variance is that a governing board cannot possibly anticipate every circumstance that will arise in the implementation of zoning and that an administrative tool short of amending the ordinance or going to court is needed to deal with these peculiar situations.

Granting an individual an exemption from the legal requirements that apply to everyone else in the city or county goes contrary to the usual presumption that the law must apply to everyone equally. Allowing variances also runs the risk that the purposes of the ordinance will, case by case, be undone. There is also the potential for abuse—that some individuals will get special treatment not available to all other landowners. Thus the statutes and the courts have imposed strict requirements on variances to make sure this tool is not abused. It is difficult to meet the legal tests to get a variance, and this difficulty is intentional. Variances are not to be routinely and easily granted. They are designed to deal with unusual and peculiar situations, not to be an ad hoc, shorthand way of amending the ordinance.

Mandatory Variance Standards

The zoning statutes allow variance requests to be considered only when the board concludes that "unnecessary hardships" would result from a strict application of the zoning requirements. If a person can comply with zoning requirements, the fact that he or she does not want to comply or that it is inconvenient or costly to comply is not a legitimate basis for a variance petition. Such costs or inconveniences are, as Justice (later Senator) Sam Ervin noted in a 1949 North Carolina Supreme Court opinion, a misfortune all property owners suffer as members of a civilized society.[1]

A local government has the option of providing flexibility to its zoning ordinance in non-hardship situations. For example, the standards could be written to allow the zoning administrator to allow up to a 10 percent allowance from required setbacks in specified circumstances, or a special use permit could be authorized if discretionary standards are involved. But if there is no unnecessary hardship, the variance tool is not available to provide flexibility.

To qualify for a variance, the applicant must show some real *unnecessary* hardship. Determining how large a hardship has to be before it becomes "unnecessary" is a case-by-case judgment—perhaps the single most difficult task for many boards handling variance requests. There is simply no hard and fast rule that can be laid down for making these decisions. The statutes stipulate that the following guidelines be used by the board as it determines whether a hardship is unnecessary:

1. The hardship results from the strict application of the ordinance. The applicant does not have to demonstrate that no reasonable use can be made of the property without the variance, a standard stated in some older ordinances.
2. The hardship must result from conditions peculiar to the specific site involved, such as its location, size, or topography. Conditions common to the neighborhood or general public cannot be the basis for granting a variance.
3. The personal circumstances of the landowner, as opposed to factors concerning the property involved, cannot be the basis for a variance.
4. The hardship must not be of the applicant or landowner's own making (often referred to as a "self-created hardship"). Purchasing property with knowledge that circumstances exist that may justify a variance is not considered a self-created hardship.

In addition to consideration of unnecessary hardship, the statutes further provide that variances can be granted only if the spirit of the ordinance is observed, public safety and welfare are secured, and substantial justice is done. This limits the scope of legally permissible variances. It is not legal, for instance, to issue a variance to allow a land use that is clearly not allowed in a particular zoning district, such as a business use in an exclusively residential zoning district. Such an unpermitted use cannot be consistent with the spirit and intent of the ordinance. The North Carolina zoning statutes specifically prohibit use variance. If someone wants to undertake a use not allowed by the zoning ordinance, he or she must ask for an amendment to the ordinance rather than a variance. Similarly, variances cannot be issued to extend or expand nonconformities, those land uses in place before the adoption of a zoning requirement that do not comply with that requirement. They also may not be issued for projects that would create a nuisance.

Members of boards making variance decisions must be careful not to substitute their judgment for what the zoning ordinance should be for that of the elected officials who are responsible for adoption and amendment of the ordinance (and for following all of the public notice and hearing requirements for ordinance amendments). If the board concludes an ordinance provision is unduly restrictive, the board can recommend amendment of the ordinance, but it is not free to issue a variance unless the strict standards of the law are met.

As with special or conditional use permits, individual variances can be granted subject to conditions. For example, the board may grant a variance to allow a parking area to be located closer than usual to the side property line but may add a condition that a fence or vegetated buffer be provided to screen the site and prevent harm to the neighbors. Any condition must be reasonably related to the variance and the standards for its approval.

Note

1. Kinney v. Sutton, 230 N.C. 404 (1949). For further information on variance law and practice, see DAVID W. OWENS, A SURVEY OF EXPERIENCE WITH ZONING VARIANCES (Special Series No. 18, Feb. 2004).

Chapter 12

Administrative Appeals and Interpretations

Zoning ordinances and other development regulations usually allow those who disagree with a staff determination on how the ordinance is interpreted or applied to make an administrative appeal of that determination to a citizen board. These appeals are usually assigned to the board of adjustment, though they can also be assigned to the planning board or governing board. A local government can also establish specialized boards to hear technical appeals of various development ordinances.

Administrative appeals are quasi-judicial decisions and must follow all of the procedural standards set out in Chapter 8, including an evidentiary hearing on each case.

Administrative Appeals

Most development regulations allow citizens to appeal administrative zoning decisions to a citizen board, typically the board of adjustment. This appeal system provides a faster, more expert review than would be the case if persons had to go directly to the courts to challenge these decisions. Such appeals may, for example, contest a notice of violation or a zoning officer's determination about whether a particular use is allowed in a particular zoning district. This is generally referred to as an "administrative" appeal, as distinct from a "judicial" appeal. Because the statutes authorize these administrative appeals, citizens must make them prior to seeking judicial review. This requirement, generally referred to as "exhausting administrative remedies," is a precondition for being able to go to court.

The administrative appeals system applies only to final, binding staff decisions or interpretations that have legal effect for a property owner or neighbor. Sometimes there is a fine line between decisions that can be appealed and those that cannot. For example, a letter from the staff confirming the existing zoning for a parcel is not appealable because it is just a statement of what the ordinance currently provides. On the other hand, a letter making a binding determination interpreting the ordinance to find that a particular use is prohibited on a site is an appealable final determination.

Boards do not have the jurisdiction to issue advisory decisions. Only binding final staff decisions or rulings may be appealed to the board.

A citizen whose application on a quasi-judicial matter has been denied by one citizen board under normal circumstances cannot appeal to a different citizen board. Quasi-judicial decisions are appealed directly to superior court. For example, if an affected party is dissatisfied with the city council's decision regarding a special use permit, that party cannot appeal the decision to the board of adjustment. The appeal must go to the courts.

Notice of Decisions and Timing of Appeals

When the staff makes a final, binding determination, notice of that decision must be provided in writing to the owner of the affected property and to the person who requested the determination (if that person was not the landowner). The notice can be delivered personally, by email, or by first-class mail. The owner and any other person with standing then has thirty days from receipt of the written notice to appeal to the board of adjustment. The appeal is filed with the city or county clerk.

Since only the landowner and the person requesting the determination automatically get a personal notice of the decision, a question arises as to when the thirty-day period to appeal starts to run for other parties (those who are directly and substantially affected by the decision and thus have standing to appeal). The period to appeal for these persons begins to run when they have actual or constructive notice of the determination. The owner receiving the determination has the option of prominently posting the affected site with a sign notifying neighbors that a zoning or subdivision decision has been made. Provided it remains up at least ten days, the sign is deemed to be constructive notice of the decision as of the date it was initially posted. The owner posting the sign must verify the posting to the zoning official who made the determination. Other typical means by which constructive notice is provided to neighbors are initiation of site preparation, delivery of construction materials to the site, or other work that would clearly indicate that the requested determination had been made.

Appeal Process

An administrative appeal must follow all of the procedures for a quasi-judicial decision set out in Chapter 8. The statutes provide a few additional requirements for appeals of staff determinations.

The appeal is initiated by filing a notice of appeal with the city clerk. The notice should state the grounds for the appeal. Issues not included in the notice of appeal may be raised for the first time at the hearing of the appeal, but if adding an issue at that time would unfairly prejudice the government or any party, the board must continue the hearing to allow all parties an adequate opportunity to prepare and respond.

Once an appeal is made, the zoning administrator transmits to the board all documents and exhibits relative to the determination being appealed. A copy of this decision record must also be transmitted to the person making the appeal and to the property owner (if that is not the person making the appeal). The official who made the decision being appealed is directed to be present at the hearing to serve as a witness and to answer any questions from a party or the board regarding the determination. The board is directed to make its decision within a reasonable time.

In a few instances, the board hearing the appeal is acting much like an appeals court. An appeal to the board of adjustment of a decision on a certificate of appropriateness made by a historic district commission is a good example. In this particular type of appeal, the board does not take any new evidence. Rather, it reviews the record of the decision created by the board previously hearing the matter in the same way a superior court reviews decisions of the board of adjustment.

In all appeals, the parties may agree to mediation or other forms of alternative dispute resolution prior to board consideration of the appeal. Local ordinances are allowed to set standards and procedures to facilitate these alternative forms of dispute resolution.

Standards for Ordinance Interpretation

A board hearing an appeal of a staff interpretation makes its own determinations and is not required to defer to the original interpretation. The board should give due consideration to past staff interpretations of the ordinance, particularly when they have been thoughtfully considered and consistently applied, but a staff interpretation is not binding.

The general rules of statutory construction apply in the interpretation of ordinance provisions or terms of individual permits for both the board of adjustment hearing an administrative appeal and for courts hearing a subsequent judicial appeal. The principal consideration in interpretation is to give effect to the intent of the legislative body that enacted the provision. Intent is determined by examining the language used, the problems it attempts to address, and the purpose or goal of the regulation. An ordinance can also provide clues to the intentions of the adopting body. For example, the ordinance may include not only definitions but also specific rules of construction (such as directing that if there is a conflict between two applicable regulations, the more restrictive one should be applied).

Beyond ascertaining intent, a board of adjustment and the courts apply standard rules of construction for ordinances and statutes in their interpretations. Among the key rules are the following:

- Where clear, plain, and unambiguous language is used, it controls.
- The common, ordinary meanings of nontechnical words should be applied unless the ordinance specifically defines a term, in which case the stated meaning must be applied. Dictionary definitions are an appropriate and standard guide for the meaning of undefined terms.
- All terms within a provision and all provisions within an ordinance must be considered, and all should be considered as a whole.
- The ordinance should be interpreted in a manner that avoids absurd consequences.
- If possible, an interpretation should be made that reconciles conflicts between sections.
- If reconciliation of conflicting sections is not possible, the latter enacted provision generally prevails, and a more specific provision controls over a more general one.
- When the ordinance restricts property rights, restrictions not clearly included within the ordinance should not be implied.

On occasion specialized rules of construction are used to make particular interpretations. The doctrine of *ejusdem generis* provides that when an enumeration of specific words is followed by general words or terms, the general term should be read to refer to the same classification as the specific terms. For example, if an ordinance requires that a parking space must be provided in a "garage or other satisfactory automobile storage space," the "other space" must be an off-street parking space similar to a garage. This rule should be applied only if the specific words in the list are part of a related series.

A similar specialized rule of construction is *expressio unius est exclusio alterius*: the mention of an express item implies the exclusion of others. For example, if the ordinance says a buffer requirement can be met by method A, B, or C, the implication is that method D is not allowed. If, however, the list is prefaced by terminology such as "including" or "including, but not limited to," that phrasing is deemed to express a legislative intent *not* to exclude other items from the list.

Chapter 13

Vested Rights and Nonconformities

Once a development regulation is adopted, the expectation is that it will apply equally to everyone. This notion of equal treatment of all persons is an important part of our legal system. Development regulations are not, however, applied to a blank slate. In a real community, there are developments already in place that are inconsistent with the rules adopted for future development, such as a preexisting store located in an area zoned for residential uses. Other developments may have been approved under an old ordinance but be only partially completed when new requirements become effective.

The courts and many development regulations make special provisions for existing and partially completed developments. The courts do this through the vested rights concept, a doctrine that provides that once a person has established a legal right to carry out a project, it can be done under the rules that were in effect when the project was approved. Development regulations, particularly zoning ordinances, also usually include provisions to handle nonconformities, preexisting uses that do not match current rules. Such provisions allow nonconformities to remain in place with limits as to future expansion.

An important consideration in this area is determining just when ordinance amendments take legal effect. The general rule is that the ordinance in effect on the day of a regulatory decision (as opposed to the day of a permit application) is the one that should be applied. Local governments have the option when amending their ordinances of postponing the effective date of the amendment or providing that it applies only to applications received after a certain date. Whether or not to do this is a policy choice for the governing board.

Vested Rights

The process of moving from an idea to develop property to the point where the development is actually finished takes time. At some point in this process, the owner obtains a legal right to continue to develop even if the rules regarding the development change. When this right is obtained, the owner is said to have a "vested right," the legal right to complete the development under the terms of the original approval.

In North Carolina land use law, there are four ways to establish a vested right. The first, established by the courts, is the *common law* vested right. The second, established by the legislature in 1985, is the *building permit* vested right. The third, established by the legislature in 1990, is the *site-specific development plan* and the *phased development plan* vested right. The fourth, established by the legislature in 2005, is through an approved *development agreement*. The means to obtain these rights are summarized in Table 13.1.

These different means of securing vested rights are not mutually exclusive. A person can have a building permit vested right that later becomes a common law vested right once substantial work is started on the project.

Common Law

The common law vested right is based on the simple principle of fairness. If a person comes to the government and gets approval to develop a project and then, in reliance on that approval, takes substantial steps to carry out the project, it would be unfair to make the person comply with newly adopted standards if doing so would cause significant hardship to that person.

In a long series of cases, the courts have developed rules for determining if and when a common law vested right has been established. The rule is that to have a common law vested right, the owner must have made substantial expenditures in good faith reliance on a valid governmental approval and suffer harm if required to comply with new standards. Each of these requirements must be met.

Table 13.1   Requirements to Obtain Vested Rights

Type of Vested Right	Requirements	Duration
Common law vested right	Substantial expenditure of time, effort, or money in good-faith reliance on a valid governmental approval and detriment if compliance required	Indefinite, likely a "reasonable" period
Building permit vested right	A valid, current building permit for the project	Generally lasts only six months unless work actually starts
Site-specific development plan vested right	A public hearing on the project, followed by local government approval of a "site-specific development plan" as defined in the zoning ordinance	Lasts at least two years; local ordinance may extend up to five years
Phased development plan vested right (optional)	General concept plan for development; may require subsequent site-specific development plan for each phase	Lasts up to five years, depending on local ordinance
Development agreement vested right (optional)	A public hearing, followed by local government approval of a detailed contractual agreement	Lasts up to twenty years, depending on individual agreement

1. *Obtain valid governmental approval.* The first step in securing a common law vested right is obtaining a valid governmental approval of a specific project.

   An owner cannot obtain a vested right by relying on the ordinance itself. Only the specific governmental approval of an individual project triggers this legal right. For example, an investor may carefully review the zoning ordinance to identify land zoned for commercial uses and then, relying on the ordinance, buy commercially zoned land, paying a substantial price for that land. The investor may even secure a letter from the staff confirming what uses are allowed by the current ordinance. But if the investor takes no action to get a specific required governmental approval to actually develop the site for a specific commercial use, and the local government subsequently rezones the land to residential use, the investor has no vested right to commercial use of the property.

"Specific governmental approval" can consist of a certificate of zoning compliance for a permitted use, a special or conditional use permit, a subdivision plat approval, a building permit, or some other required approval. Staff advice or assurance that approval will be forthcoming is not sufficient, as the approval required must be a formal determination or mandatory approval. The approval that is received must be valid at the time received—vested rights cannot be based on a mistakenly or illegally granted permit. The requirement of specific governmental approval is waived only if no permit was required for the proposed development and the owner was proceeding in an entirely lawful manner. In such a case, a common law vested right can be established if the other parts of the rule are met.

2. *Make a substantial expenditure.* The second step in securing a common law vested right is to make some substantial expenditure after receiving a specific governmental approval. The expenditure must be made in reliance on the approval, not in anticipation of it. Expenditures made prior to approval and those made to secure approval do not count. The expenditure can be of time, effort, or money. Actual construction is not necessary. The expenditure must be "substantial" in relation to the overall expenditure required to carry out the project. For example, simply going to the site and making some modest site clearing or construction may not be a "substantial" expenditure for a large commercial project, but a few hours' work toward installing a billboard may be sufficient if that brings the job close to completion. If the project is being carried out in several phases, the vested right will apply only to those phases for which the expenditures have actually been made.

3. *Act in good faith.* Equity and fairness must be considered: the owner must have been acting in good faith. If it is apparent that the owner was deceiving or misleading the government or neighbors, or if the owner was acting outside of normal business practices, such as moving with undue haste in order to beat a rule change, a common law vested right is not established.

4. *Suffer harm.* The owner must show that he or she would be harmed if required to comply with the new rules. If all of the expenditures made under the original approval can be applied just as well to a project that complies with the new rules, there is no vested right to develop under the old rules.

The next two vested rights were created by the legislature in an attempt to bring greater certainty and simplicity to this question.

Building Permit

The building permit vested right became a provision of the zoning enabling statutes in 1985 in Sections 153A-344(b) and 160A-385(b) of the North Carolina General Statutes (hereinafter G.S.). It provides that as long as a valid building permit is outstanding, the owner has a vested right to complete the development authorized by that permit. There is no requirement that any expenditures be made in reliance on the building permit. The permit involved here is not just any permit; it must be the building permit required under the state building code. These building permits expire six months after issuance if work has not commenced. They also expire after work commences if there is a twelve-month period of no work. Building permits may also be revoked for any substantial departure from the approved plans, failure to comply with any applicable state or local law (not just the building code and zoning ordinance), and any misrepresentations made in securing the permit. Building permits mistakenly issued may also be revoked, but there is not a legal mandate to do so. If the building permit expires or is revoked, the vested right based on it is also lost.

Site-Specific or Phased Development Plan

The second statutory vested right is the site-specific or phased development plan, which was added to the statutes in 1990 to deal with more complex development projects (G.S. 153A-344.1 and G.S. 160A-385.1). Each local government is allowed to establish in its zoning ordinance its own definition of what constitutes a site-specific development plan. For the purposes of securing a vested right, a "site plan" is not necessarily the same thing as a "site-specific development plan." Site-specific development plans may include preliminary plats under subdivision ordinances as well as conditional and special use permits. If the local zoning ordinance itself does not define site-specific development plans, an owner can use any zoning permit to qualify.

Does This New Zoning Apply to Me? The *Smith* Case

In the spring of 1968, Dupree Smith decided Hillsborough needed a new dry cleaning establishment. Smith's proposal triggered a zoning fight somewhat reminiscent of the struggle forty years earlier in the *Aydlett* case described in Chapter 4.

At the time Smith started planning his business, the town had no zoning. A plan to enact zoning had been discussed several years earlier, but not enacted. However, the planning board had been hard at work on a new zoning ordinance for about a year. In March 1968 Smith paid $100 for an option to purchase a lot for his business on Churton Street, the town's main street. There was a two-story house occupied by a renter on the lot, which was in a residential area a few blocks north of the courthouse and the town's small business district. The lot involved was owned by a local businessman who was also a member of the town planning board.

In April the planning board recommended a zoning ordinance that placed most of the town (including the lot Smith was considering for his business) in a residential zoning district. At this point Smith visited the mayor and discussed his plans; the mayor later testified he told Smith about the pending zoning at this meeting and even gave him a copy of the draft ordinance. Smith acknowledged the meeting, but said they only talked about a building permit, and he denied that zoning came up in the conversation.

A rapid series of events ensued in May. On May 2 the first required newspaper ad ran, noting the town board would hold a hearing on zoning adoption on May 27. A news story in the same edition of the local paper, the *News of Orange County*, noted most of the town would be placed in a residential zoning district. The next day, May 3, Smith got a building permit for his dry cleaning business. The long-time town clerk later testified she told Smith about the impending zoning at this time; Smith again denied that zoning was ever mentioned; and the building inspector (a neighbor of Smith's) testified he did not mention zoning to Smith when the building permit was issued. On May 9 the local paper ran a large front page story on the proposed zoning, included a copy of the proposed zoning map, and ran an editorial supporting zoning. On May 16 the second required legal ad ran in the paper. On May 22 Smith closed on his purchase of the property, paying $9,500 for the lot. The same day he entered a contract for the construction of a metal building on the site, paying about half the $15,000 construction cost as a down payment. The following day, May 23, Smith staked the structure's location on the site. On May 27 the town held its public hearing. The hearing took only a half hour instead of the two and a half hours scheduled as

The local government must conduct a hearing before approving a site-specific development plan. This should probably be an evidentiary hearing, but the statutes are unclear on this point. Once the plan is approved, the owner's vested right is established; the owner is protected from future zoning changes that affect the type or intensity of development that has already been approved. The site-specific development plan vested right is good for two years (individual local governments have the option of extending this only twelve persons showed up to speak and no major objections were raised. Smith did not attend the hearing. At the close of the hearing the town council unanimously adopted the ordinance and made it effective immediately.

Since construction of the building had not commenced, the town took the view that the new zoning applied to Smith's project and that a commercial structure could not be built on the site since it was now zoned for residential use only. Smith took the view that he had proceeded far enough that he could legally continue. So on June 5 he entered a franchise agreement for a dry cleaning business and made a contract for equipment purchase. On June 11 the town sent him a notice revoking the building permit and the battle was joined. On July 8 Smith pressed ahead and had the house on the lot demolished and the lot graded. The town sued him on July 11 and got a restraining order preventing further work on the site. At the end of July the town and Smith agreed that he could landscape the lot pending the court hearing, but he was not allowed to unload the prefabricated building he had purchased.

The case went to a day-and-a-half jury trial in late September. There was conflicting testimony about what Smith knew and when he knew it. The mayor and town clerk testified they had personally advised Smith his project was inconsistent with the pending zoning prior to the building permit being issued. Smith testified he was aware there was some general discussion of zoning going on, but he thought all the

continued

This single-family home was eventually built on the same site proposed for a dry cleaners in downtown Hillsborough.

to as much as five years). The availability of this two-year vested right under a site-specific development plan is mandatory for all North Carolina cities and counties. It exists even if not mentioned in a particular ordinance.

In a variation on this process, owners may submit and local governments may approve a more general phased development plan that gives this same type of vested right for up to five years. A phased development plan is a more general depiction of proposed development over a longer time. A local press coverage was about zoning in Chapel Hill (which is about ten miles south of Hillsborough). Smith swore he was unaware that zoning might affect his project until his permit was revoked. The jury found Smith had acted in good faith and had made a substantial investment prior to the adoption of zoning, so the court held he had a right to continue with his construction.

The town promptly appealed and construction continued on hold. In May 1969, a year after the dispute began, the state court of appeals held the evidence on exactly when Smith learned of the proposed zoning was unclear and ordered a new trial. This ruling was appealed to the state supreme court, and the delay continued.

In December 1969, in a landmark ruling on vested rights, the state supreme court held that Smith had indeed established a legal right to proceed.[a] The court held that if substantial expenditures have been made in reliance on an approval, there need not be actual construction on site to get a vested right. Here the purchase of the land and the contracts for a building and equipment were all done after the building permit had been issued. The court held that if Smith had acted in haste with knowledge of the impending zoning in a race to beat the effective date of the ordinance, he would have no good faith and thus no vested right; but the jury's conclusion that he acted in good faith was conclusive and the town would not be allowed to apply its zoning to this project.

So what happened as a result? For one thing, the state law on vested rights was amended in 1985 to clarify that if a person has a building permit, he or she has a vested right to build as long as that permit is valid, thus putting an end to debate about whether there was "good faith" or whether a particular expenditure was "substantial" in those instances where a building permit exists (though in the *Smith* case, the building permit had been revoked a month after it was issued).

And the site in question? The metal building for a dry cleaners was never built. Smith later sold the lot rather than build on it. A single-family residence, fully consistent with the town zoning, was later built on the site (see photo on page 139). The town further helped protect the character of this part of downtown in 1972 by buying the small historic house across the street, which had been vacant for fifty years, and renovating it as the new town hall.

---

a. Town of Hillsborough v. Smith, 276 N.C. 48 (1969).

government must provide for a site-specific development plan vested right, but the phased development plan is optional.

Development Agreements

In 2005 North Carolina authorized use of development agreements. The use of this tool is optional for each city and county. A city or county is authorized to enter into these agreements with a landowner to provide that the existing local development regulations will remain effective for that property for a period of up to twenty years. The minimum land size for an individual agreement is 25 developable acres. The statutes have detailed requirements for the contents of these agreements. Each individual development agreement must be adopted as an ordinance by the local government, with the same notice and hearing as required for a zoning text amendment. The agreement must also include a description of any new public facilities that will serve the development, specify who will provide these facilities, and set out when the facilities will be provided. All approved development agreements must be recorded in the chain of title for the affected property.

Nonconformities

Virtually all zoning ordinances include provisions that allow continuation of existing development that is inconsistent with the terms of the new ordinance. Such developments are called nonconformities. Protections may extend to several types of nonconformities: a nonconforming use, such as a business in a residential district; a nonconforming lot, such as one that is smaller than the minimum allowed in a particular district; or a nonconforming structure, such as one that is too close to the rear property line.

A nonconformity must have been legal when it was initiated to receive protection. A use that was a zoning violation when it started does not ripen into a legitimate nonconformity no matter how long it has been there. If the original approval was issued in error and later revoked, the offending use or structure is not a legal nonconformity.

If there is a dispute as to when the nonconformity was established or what its scope is, the zoning administrator considers the evidence and makes a ruling on the question. The burden is on the person claiming a nonconformity to establish that it was in fact in existence and what its scope was when it became nonconforming. Appeals of the zoning administrator's determination in this matter can be taken to the board of adjustment.

Most ordinances allow nonconformities to continue but to place limitations on them. The scope of these limitations varies with each ordinance. Most zoning ordinances limit nonconformities with the intent of eventually phasing them out or at least keeping them from getting any worse. A typical restriction is that a nonconforming building cannot be enlarged, expanded, or extended. *Expansion* is usually defined to include additions to structures. It can also include improvements that increase or extend the

Can We Ever Get Rid of This Junkyard? The *Joyner* Case

Jurisdictions can phase out nonconformities through amortization, but sometimes these uses turn out to be quite persistent. The North Carolina court case that established the law on amortization is a good example.

In 1966 Roy Joyner started a building salvage yard on property he leased in north Winston-Salem. A city zoning provision adopted in 1968 required this salvage yard to be removed within three years. Joyner contended it would cost him $25,000 to relocate and refused to comply. In 1973 the city cited him for a criminal violation of the zoning ordinance. At trial, the jury found him guilty, and this verdict was upheld by both the North Carolina and United States supreme courts. The state supreme court decision, written by Justice (and former governor) Dan Moore, concluded that amortization is legal so long as the time allowed to come into compliance is reasonable.[a]

The *Joyner* case authorized removal of this small junkyard.

So, after all of this lengthy legal wrangling and a trip to the highest courts, what happened to Joyner's salvage yard? It continued operation on the same site for decades (see photo above). After the city won in court, it agreed to rezone the property to a district that would allow continuation of the salvage yard.

---

a. State v. Joyner, 286 N.C. 366, *appeal dismissed*, 422 U.S. 1002 (1975).

commercial viability of a nonconforming use. Another limit is that a nonconforming use cannot be resumed if it has been abandoned or discontinued for a specified period (typically six to twelve months). There are often restrictions on repairs of nonconforming structures. Routine maintenance and minor repairs are usually allowed, but substantial repairs or replacement are not. An ordinance with this type of restriction should carefully define the boundary between permissible repairs and impermissible replacement (such as forbidding renovations that cost more than 50 percent of the current value of a nonconforming structure). The ordinance also often prohibits the owner from changing one nonconforming use to a different nonconforming use.

There are important factors cities and counties should consider in adopting limits on nonconformities. How much impact will the continuing nonconformity have on the interests protected by the current regulation? How will the limits affect the owner of the nonconformity? What is the appropriate balance between the interests of landowners who must comply with the current regulations and the rights of those who undertook action some time ago in a completely lawful fashion?

Restrictions on nonconformities are legal and enforceable. However, if there is any doubt as to whether a restriction applies, the courts resolve that doubt in favor of allowing the person to make continued use of the property as it exists. Therefore local governments should carefully consider just how restrictive they want the nonconforming limitations to be and clearly define those limits in the ordinance.

In some limited circumstances, a local government can require a nonconformity to be terminated (removed) or force the owner to bring the use into compliance with the ordinance. If the nonconformity poses a threat to public health and safety, immediate termination is warranted. For example, a new regulation preventing signs that block sight lines at intersections may require all offending signs to be removed immediately to prevent accidents and protect public safety. Otherwise, an owner must be given a reasonable amount of time to recoup his or her investment and make alternate plans before having to come into compliance. The practice of requiring inconsistent uses to be phased out or brought into compliance after a defined grace period is called *amortization* and is necessary to prevent the requirement to bring the nonconformity into compliance from being an unconstitutional taking of private property. For example, a billboard owner may be given five years to use a nonconforming billboard, but at the end of the amortization period it must be brought into compliance (such as replacing it with a smaller sign, if that is allowed, or removing it altogether). The amortization period allowed must be reasonable in light of the owner's investment in the nonconformity, the income it generates, its salvage value, and the like. The amortization tool has been applied most often in North Carolina to signs, junkyards, and adult entertainment uses. Federal and state statutes now limit the use of amortization of off-premise advertising signs (see Chapter 14).

Chapter 14

Statutory Limitations on Local Powers

For the most part, decisions about what land uses to regulate and how to do so are left to the discretion of local elected officials. However, since zoning and other development regulations are powers delegated from the state to local governments, the state can impose limits on local regulatory authority in order to address statewide concerns. Federal legislation also increasingly limits local discretion regarding development regulation.

The state or federal government can override local regulations in two ways. First, it can decide to regulate a certain topic by itself, thereby preempting any local regulation of that matter. For example, federal construction standards for manufactured homes override any state or local building code standards covering manufactured homes. Likewise, the state building code precludes any local construction standards for site-built buildings. Federal or state preemption is sometimes explicitly stated in the law. Even when it is not stated, however, preemption is implied if the courts conclude a state or federal law so completely addresses a subject as to fully occupy the field of potential regulation. The second way state or federal legislation controls local regulations is by mandating how the local regulation is to be carried out. For example, the state mandates that local zoning not completely exclude manufactured homes from an entire jurisdiction but allows zoning ordinances to regulate the location, dimensions, and appearance of such homes.

Following are brief summaries of some of the key state and federal statutory limits on local development regulation.

Agricultural operations are exempt from county (but not city) zoning.

Agriculture

The North Carolina zoning enabling statutes exempt most agricultural operations from county zoning. This exemption does not apply to zoning by cities within city boundaries, but farming in a city's extraterritorial area is exempt from city development regulation.

Only "bona fide farm" operations are exempt. For the purposes of this exemption, farm operations include growing crops, raising livestock and poultry, growing plants in a greenhouse or nursery, tree farming, aquaculture, and agritourism. Local governments must accept any of the following evidence that land is being used for farm purposes: a farm sales tax exemption certificate, present use value taxation for property taxes, federal income tax Schedule F, a forestry management plan, or a farm identification number from the U.S. Department of Agriculture.

The exemption does not apply to most commercial operations related to agriculture, such as a store selling fertilizer or a meat-packing operation. Grain-drying and grain storage operations, however, are expressly made part of the exempt farming operations by state law. Also, limited commercial activity incidental to an exempt farming activity is exempt, such as a farm having a roadside produce stand. The farm exemptions do not extend to nonfarm use of farms, such as placing a residence for a nonfarm worker on a farm, operating a dog kennel, or producing biofuels. Also, county zoning may regulate large-scale hog farms (those with over 600,000 pounds of swine on-site).

Counties are also prohibited from using zoning to prohibit single-family residences on lots exceeding 10 acres in zoning districts where more than half the land is used for farming or forestry.

Alcohol Sales

The North Carolina courts have ruled that a state ABC permit overrides local zoning ordinances. When a person applies for an ABC permit to sell beer, wine, or mixed drinks, the permit application is circulated to local governments, who can comment as to whether the proposal is compatible with local zoning. The state ABC Board is required to consider these comments, but is not required to follow them. If a permit is issued, the person can do what the ABC permit allows even if it is inconsistent with zoning.

Some local governments attempt to impose restrictions on alcohol sales in permitted facilities. Examples have included prohibiting a nonconforming restaurant in a residential district from selling alcohol or issuing a special use permit that purports to limit the hours a convenience store can sell beer. If the facility gets an ABC permit, such restrictions are preempted by state regulations and are not enforceable through local zoning. Local regulations or permit conditions that are not related to alcohol sales, such as landscaping or parking requirements, are likely not preempted and should be legally enforceable.

Family Care Homes

Family care homes are facilities that provide health, counseling, or related services to a small number of persons in a family environment. Both state and federal laws affect zoning regulation of these facilities.

Under North Carolina law, a zoning ordinance must treat family care homes the same as it treats single-family residences. They cannot be prohibited in a district that allows a single-family residence nor can they be subject to any special review requirements, such as a special or conditional use requirement. These limitations also apply to private restrictive covenants that affect family care homes. This state law does allow zoning ordinances to require a half-mile separation between family care homes, but it is unclear if these minimum separations will always be valid under the federal Fair Housing Act (discussed below).

The terminology here can be confusing. It is important to remember that the definition of a *family care home* for zoning purposes is not the same as that for state social service licensing purposes. To qualify for zoning protection, the facility must be designed to provide room, board, and care for six or fewer handicapped persons in a family environment. *Handicapped persons* are defined by the statute to include those with temporary or permanent physical, emotional, or mental disabilities, but not those who have been deemed dangerous to themselves or to others.

The federal Fair Housing Act prohibits local governments from discriminating against persons with disabilities. This act makes it unlawful to prohibit or "otherwise make unavailable" housing for the disabled. Local governments must also make "reasonable accommodation" for housing those with disabilities. For the purposes of this statute, these protections must be afforded to those with any physical or mental impairment, including disease and substance abuse, that limits a major life function.

Exactly how much accommodation is necessary to be "reasonable" is not precisely defined by this federal law. For example, in a case involving a home for recovering alcoholics and drug addicts, the United States Supreme Court ruled that a zoning provision that limits the number of unrelated individuals who may occupy a house in a particular zoning district is subject to the Fair Housing Act.[1] (Minimum housing codes that set a minimum square footage per individual resident are exempt.) So if a zoning ordinance includes a limit on the number of individuals residing in a house (such as a requirement that not more than six unrelated individuals may occupy a home in a single-family zoning district), the local government must consider whether this is unlawful discrimination or a failure to make reasonable accommodation for handicapped persons. Requirements for minimum separations between family care homes have been upheld in the courts, but the results often depend on the exact facts involved. For example, in a particular city a minimum separation of 1,000 feet between treatment facilities in single-family neighborhoods may be deemed reasonable, while the half-mile separation allowed by state law could be determined to be a failure to make a reasonable accommodation for a particular proposed facility.

Manufactured Housing

In 1987 the state legislature directed North Carolina cities and counties to take steps to improve the supply of affordable housing. The legislation states that zoning ordinances may not completely exclude manufactured housing (the current legal term for what used to be known as mobile homes or trailers) from an entire jurisdiction.

Some zoning regulation of manufactured housing is allowed, however. Permissible restrictions include:

1. standards on location, such as allowing manufactured housing only in certain zoning districts or in mobile home parks;
2. dimensional requirements, such as allowing only double-wide units in certain zoning districts; and
3. appearance standards, such as requiring skirting be installed or requiring units to have pitched roofs. A local government cannot, however, impose regulations based on the age or market value of manufactured homes.

The above requirements apply only to units defined as manufactured homes, which are those built in a factory to federal construction standards (and having a HUD inspection sticker) rather than state building code standards. A few zoning ordinances apply similar location and appearance standards to modular homes, which are factory built but are covered by the state building code rather than federal standards. Most local development regulations, however, treat modular homes the same as conventional site-built housing. State law does establish minimum design standards for modular homes. These standards include having a pitched roof, use of exterior materials similar to those used for site-built homes, and placement of the home on a permanent foundation.

Federal law sets construction standards for manufactured housing, and a city or county may not impose additional building or safety standards through zoning. However, this limited federal preemption does not prohibit local government regulation of the appearance of manufactured housing (such as a requirement to have a pitched, shingled roof and lapped siding).

Outdoor Advertising

Federal highway laws provide that states must manage outdoor advertising along certain federally funded roads or face a 10 percent reduction in federal financial aid for highways. In response the state limits new billboards near federal highways to those areas that are either unzoned or are zoned for commercial or industrial uses. Another aspect of this federal incentive for state mandates is that local regulations are not allowed to use amortization

Many zoning ordinances restrict the location of manufactured housing and impose regulations on the appearance of such structures.

to remove nonconforming signs along certain federally funded roads—if a local government wants to remove nonconforming billboards from these areas, cash compensation to the sign owner is required (see Chapter 13 for more details on nonconformities). State law also requires monetary compensation if owners are required to remove nonconforming off-premise outdoor advertising (unless the sign is a public safety hazard, is relocated, or is removed subject to a broader requirement for removal of damaged structures).

State law also addresses placement of campaign signs in state highway rights-of-way. Cities may adopt different standards for city streets. These regulations limit the time before and after elections that signs may be displayed, limit the height and size of the signs, and require permission from adjacent landowners.

Public Buildings

In North Carolina the zoning enabling statutes provide that zoning ordinances apply to the erection, construction, and use of buildings by the state and its political subdivisions. Buildings used or constructed by state agencies, counties, cities, and utility districts must comply with zoning requirements. The associated aspects of a building (such as parking, signage, and landscaping) are also subject to zoning requirements. Governmental land uses that do not involve a building are not subject to local zoning (for example, a parking lot not associated with a regulated building).

Buildings used by the federal government are not subject to local zoning. Federal law does direct federal facilities to be consistent with local zoning "to the greatest extent practicable," but consistency is not mandatory.

Solar Collectors

State law provides that zoning regulations may not prohibit solar collectors on single-family residences. Regulations may limit location of solar structures visible from the ground if they face a public area.

Telecommunication

Both federal and state law have special provisions for telecommunication towers. These limitations balance the national interest in an effective and reliable system for wireless communication with local interests in reasonable land use regulation.

Federal law provides that a local zoning restriction cannot unreasonably discriminate among providers of similar services. Local regulations must not have the effect of totally prohibiting service in an area. Local regulations cannot be based on the environmental health effects of electromagnetic radiation.

Federal law also imposes several procedural requirements: local governments must act on applications for telecommunication towers within a reasonable time, any denials must be made in writing, there must be substantial evidence in the record to support a denial, and tower modifications that are not substantial (such as collocation of new antennae on an existing tower or minor height increases) must be approved.

It is permissible under these federal restrictions for a local ordinance to limit towers to certain zoning districts and to impose fencing, landscaping, lighting, and setback requirements. A local government may require some evidence of need for a new tower and a showing that alternate sites (other towers or structures) are not available. An ordinance may also require towers to be constructed so as to allow future location of additional antennae

This Cary telecommunications tower was disguised to blend into a pine grove along I-40.

(collocation requirements). Some ordinances also require camouflaging where feasible (sometimes referred to as "stealth towers") and provisions for removal of the tower if it is no longer in active use.

State law similarly allows local regulations to address the land use impacts of telecommunication facilities—siting, setbacks, landscaping, and similar aesthetic and safety considerations. Local governments may not, however, require information about an applicant's business decisions (but they may consider whether existing towers can adequately serve target areas). Local governments must also provide streamlined decisions on applications to collocate new antennae on existing structures and generally do so within forty-five days of receipt of complete applications. Local governments are required to expeditiously approve requests for minor modifications of existing towers for collocation of additional wireless facilities, provided the modification does not add more than 10 percent to the height of the structure or more than 20 feet to its width.

State and federal law also require that local zoning regulations reasonably accommodate amateur radio antennae. Federal rules prohibit height restrictions of less than 90 feet unless necessary to achieve a clearly defined health, safety, or aesthetic objective.

Satellite dishes are not exempt from zoning, but the federal government has limited the extent to which local governments can regulate their size and location. Local restrictions on satellite dishes smaller than one meter in diameter (and on dishes less than two meters in diameter if located in commercial or industrial zoning districts) are presumed to be unreasonable.

An historic district ordinance may preclude satellite dishes if it also precludes other exterior antennae. A zoning restriction limiting large satellite dishes to rear yards or requiring some screening is generally permissible as long as it does not cause an undue burden in a particular situation.

Watersheds and Water Quality

State law mandates local land use regulation of water supply watersheds (see Figure 14.1 for a map of affected watersheds). In 1989 the legislature mandated that those 200-plus local governments whose jurisdiction contains surface water bodies used for a public water supply adopt minimum land use regulations to protect the quality of those waters. The primary aim of these regulations is to prevent harmful runoff into the water supplies, thus protecting public health and reducing the cost of water supply (it being cheaper to prevent contamination of the water than to clean it up). The state Environmental Management Commission classifies the state's watersheds, establishing the level of protection required; sets the minimum standards for local watershed ordinances; and reviews and approves each ordinance and any significant ordinance amendments.

Watershed and water quality regulations limit certain uses, such as storage of hazardous materials or landfills near the water, and limit density of development along the shoreline that drains into these waters. The density limits for residential development take the form of minimum lot sizes; for commercial and industrial development, they put a limit on the amount of a lot that can be built on. The state rules do allow local governments to adopt a high-density option that permits more intensive development if the developer takes measures to control runoff, such as installing a pond to collect rainwater.

In addition to the water supply watersheds, state and federal regulations require local land use regulations to protect water quality. Federal law requires the state's urbanized areas to have stormwater control programs.

Figure 14.1   Watershed Regulation Ordinances in North Carolina

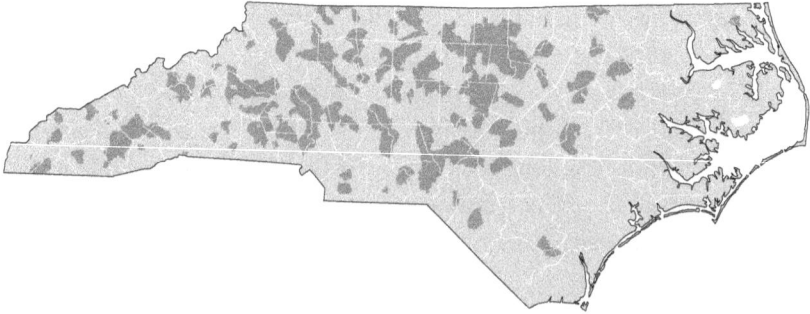

Local governments are required to adopt watershed protection ordinances in these shaded areas.

State rules implementing these programs require that the amount of built-upon area be limited and that minimum vegetated buffers be maintained along sensitive rivers and streams to reduce the harmful impacts of urban runoff.

Note

1. City of Edmonds v. Oxford House, Inc., 514 U.S. 725 (1995). The Court invalidated limits on unrelated individuals living together in *Moore v. City of East Cleveland*, 431 U.S. 494 (1977). The Court upheld limits on unrelated persons living together in *Village of Belle Terre v. Boraas*, 416 U.S. 1 (1974).

Chapter 15

Constitutional Limits

The power of local governments to regulate land use and development is subject to the limits imposed by the state and federal constitutions. Any regulatory action that is inconsistent with these limits can be declared unconstitutional by the courts and invalidated. A local government undertaking an unconstitutional action may also be subject to financial liability. Given the practical and political sensibilities of most local elected officials, it is rare that a local development regulation will violate constitutional limits. But the limits are there, they are real, and it is important to understand them. As U.S. Supreme Court Justice William Brennan remarked in reviewing the constitutionality of a land use regulation, "After all, a policeman must know the Constitution, then why not a planner?"[1]

There are three basic limits on development regulations imposed by the United States Constitution (and parallel provisions in the state constitution). These are (1) the restrictions imposed by the Due Process Clause that governmental actions be fundamentally fair, (2) the requirement of the Equal Protection Clause that persons in similar situations be treated alike by the law, and (3) the limitation of the Taking Clause that private property not be taken for public use without compensation. In addition, the First Amendment guarantees of freedom of speech and religion limit local regulatory authority relative to adult businesses, signs, and religious land uses.

Due Process

The Fifth and Fourteenth amendments to the United States Constitution provide that no person shall be deprived of life, liberty, or property without due process of law. A similar provision, the "law of the land" clause, is in the North Carolina constitution. The courts have interpreted this requirement to impose two important limitations. First, hearings and the regulatory decision-making process must be carried out fairly. Second, the substance of development regulations must be reasonable.

The first requirement of procedural fairness is relatively straightforward. Its most important application is the requirement that all hearings on quasi-judicial zoning matters—variances, special and conditional use permits, and appeals of administrator determinations—be conducted in a fair and impartial manner. Since quasi-judicial development regulation decisions involve the determination of individual legal rights in a particular case, these proceedings must be conducted somewhat similarly to a court proceeding. While some informality is allowed, North Carolina courts have held that in the zoning context due process requires that all of the fundamental rights to a fair hearing be observed. The applicant and other directly affected persons appearing at an evidentiary hearing have these rights:

- To present witnesses and documents.
- To inspect all the evidence being considered by the decision maker.
- To cross-examine witnesses at the hearings. Board members may also question witnesses.
- To have the witnesses testify under oath.
- To have the decision made solely on the basis of evidence presented at the hearing. Board members may not gather information about quasi-judicial matters except during the hearing.
- To have written findings of fact if there are disputed facts in the case.
- To have an impartial decision maker. A board member with a financial interest in the outcome of the decision may not participate in making rezonings and other legislative zoning decisions. With quasi-judicial zoning decisions, board members may not participate in a matter involving someone with whom they have a close family or business relationship, nor may they participate if they have a bias (defined as fixed opinion that is not susceptible to change upon hearing the facts at the hearing).

These procedural due process rights as applied to quasi-judicial decisions are discussed in more detail in Chapter 8.

The other aspect of due process—that development regulations be reasonable—is a bit more complicated. The courts have ruled that this requirement (referred to as "substantive due process") has two components. First, regulations must be based on legitimate governmental objectives. Second, there must be a reasonable relationship between the specific regulations and these legitimate objectives.

Legitimate governmental objectives. In determining whether a regulation is based on legitimate objectives, it is important that a city or county has completed solid technical studies and plans that can serve as the foundation for its ordinances. These studies and plans should address the area's natural features, population changes, existing development, public service needs, and the like. Examples of legitimate objectives for zoning include protecting public health and safety, assuring adequate public utilities (including transportation, water, sewer, parks, and schools), protecting natural resources and open spaces, protecting community aesthetics and historic values, and conserving and protecting property values. The courts have ruled that development regulations cannot be used to promote residential racial segregation, to control the ownership (as opposed to the use) of property, to enforce private restrictive covenants on property use, or otherwise to protect private rather than public interests.

As a general rule, courts do not review the motives of a board in adopting a regulation, reasoning that it is usually impossible to know why a board really made a particular policy choice. But there must be some rational, plausible, legitimate basis for the regulation. For example, it is legal to regulate the location of manufactured housing in order to protect neighboring property values and assure adequate provision of public services. But a restriction on manufactured housing based solely on ethnic discrimination would be invalid.

Reasonable relation. There must also be a reasonable relation between the legitimate goals of a regulation and the ordinance. In other words, each restriction must be designed to achieve a legitimate objective. For example, if a city uses zoning to prohibit a drive-through window in a fast food restaurant because of traffic problems, but allows banks and other businesses in the same zoning district to have drive-through windows, the court may well conclude there is no reasonable relation between the end (preventing traffic problems) and the means chosen (limiting drive-through windows for some but not all businesses).

Due process also dictates that an ordinance restriction not be so vague that a person would not know what it does and does not require. If the standard required in an ordinance is too general or imprecise, a court may invalidate it. For example, a requirement that signs not be "unattractive" or that a business not be "too noisy" would be too vague to pass constitutional muster.

Equal Protection

The Equal Protection Clause of the Fourteenth Amendment to the United States Constitution says that local governments cannot deny any person the equal protection of the law. This notion of the law applying evenhandedly is central to our legal system. Yet zoning ordinances clearly treat persons differently. What is permitted in one zoning district is prohibited in another district. A person who has already established a business in an area later zoned for residential use is allowed to stay, but someone else may be forbidden to open a new, similar business next door.

The Equal Protection Clause does not require everyone to be treated exactly the same. What it does require is that persons in similar situations be treated similarly. So the key question becomes: When are people similarly situated?

The courts allow different development standards in different zoning districts because there has been a conclusion by the city council that different situations exist in different parts of the city. For example, one part of the city may be well suited for residential development, so it is acceptable to zone it for residential use and impose standards suitable for a residential area that are different from the standards appropriate for an industrial area. Similarly, the person who had a development legally in place before zoning was adopted is in a different situation from the person wanting to develop after the ordinance is in place. Or, a place of worship may be exempted from the off-street parking requirements that apply to a business because it usually has a large parking demand only at times outside of normal business hours. In each of these instances of different treatment, the key is that there be a real and meaningful difference between the parties being treated differently.

A special cautionary note must be applied here. If a case-specific zoning restriction affects an owner's fundamental constitutionally protected rights, such as the right of free speech, and that person takes the government to court to challenge the restrictions, the government must convince the court that there is a compelling reason for the special restriction, something that is almost impossible to do in a development regulation context. For example, the Supreme Court said a city cannot prohibit news racks that sell sexually oriented papers while allowing similar news racks selling regular newspapers.[2] The same exacting limitation applies to restrictions based on a constitutionally suspect classification, such as different treatment based on race, religion, or national origin. For example, a zoning restriction that limited occupancy in a particular residential district to a particular race would be invalid.

Taking

The Fifth Amendment dictates that when private property is taken for public use, the owner must be fairly paid for the property. This was a simple proposition as long as it was applied to those instances where the government actually took title to or possession of private property, such as taking a person's land to build a road, a school, or a military base. Usually the only question in those instances was how much the land was worth and what would be just or fair compensation.

The legal situation as it relates to development regulation got considerably more complicated when the United States Supreme Court ruled in 1922 that a regulation that restricts property use could be so onerous that it has the same practical effect as a seizure of property.[3] Thus, an individual property owner could not be singled out to bear a burden that should be borne by the public as a whole. Moving beyond this general concept to its application has proved difficult. The notion that an overly restrictive regulation can be a taking of property has become one of the most hotly contested and legally confusing areas of land use law.

With more than a dozen United States Supreme Court decisions on this topic in recent decades, a few rules have emerged. First, a restriction that requires a physical invasion of a person's property is automatically a taking. For example, regulatory requirements that the public be allowed to use a private boat basin and that apartment building owners be required to allow cable TV wiring on their roof have both been held to be takings.[4] Second, a regulation that renders a property completely worthless is a taking.[5] For there to be an automatic taking, the regulation must remove *all* practical use of the property so that it has no reasonable value left.

If a case does not fit into one of these two rather narrow categories, the courts conduct an individual review of the case to determine if a regulation has gone too far and is thus unconstitutional.[6] An important factor in these reviews is the economic impact on the person affected, with particular emphasis on the impact on "distinct investment-backed expectations." The character of the governmental action is also an important factor. A land use restriction enacted to protect public health and safety is far less likely to be a taking than one adopted for improper purposes, such as to reduce the value of the property as a prelude to public purchase. A severe reduction in value, such as might occur when a property is rezoned from a valuable commercial use to a less valuable residential use, is not itself a taking if the regulation permitted any practical use remaining under the regulation that has some economic value.

It is extremely unusual for the courts to hold that a local development restriction is a taking. Most local governments reach the political limits of what they deem to be fair and reasonable well before they get close to constitutional limits. But the uncertainty of the law in this area has provoked a great deal of controversy, debate, and litigation.

Two other areas of taking law warrant mention. The first is amortization, the practice of requiring nonconforming uses to be phased out or brought into compliance within a specified period. The courts in North Carolina have ruled that this is not a taking as long as a reasonable time period is allowed before requiring compliance.[7] The length of the period should be based on the amount of the investment in the use, the time it takes to recoup that investment, and the time needed to make alternative plans for use of the property. The courts have approved a five-year period for the removal of nonconforming billboards and a three-year period for the screening or removal of a nonconforming junkyard. There are, however, statutory (as opposed to constitutional) limits on the use of amortization. For example, federal highway laws effectively prevent the use of amortization to compel removal of nonconforming billboards along federal highways. (See Chapter 14 for more details on this limit).

Second, many zoning and subdivision ordinances require land developers to make dedications to the public—often called "exactions"—as a condition of development approval. For example, there may be a requirement that streets and utilities be provided by the developer and turned over to the government. These requirements are legal so long as there is clear statutory authority to impose the exactions, the exactions are necessary to meet a legitimate governmental objective and reasonably related to those objectives, and the size or amount of the exactions are roughly proportional to the impacts of that development.[8] These limitations apply to land dedications, construction requirements, and payment of money. For example, it is perfectly legitimate to require a developer to pave and dedicate to the public all internal streets within a new subdivision, to install utility lines to all lots being developed, or to contribute money to a park fund to build the recreation facilities needed by these new residents. All of these exactions are needed to address public impacts created by the proposed development. But it would be impermissible to require as a condition of government approval of a subdivision that the developer of a very small subdivision build a major highway to serve the entire city (because the size of the exaction is well out of proportion to the impacts of the proposed development).

Beyond the constitutional limitation on exactions, there must be an explicit legislative authorization for any exaction proposed by a local government. State statutes specifically authorize several types of exactions, including securing rights-of-way and construction of streets and utility lines, securing parks and open space, and constructing other community service facilities. As for schools, a new subdivision may be required to reserve a site for future governmental purchase, but there is no authority to require payment for construction of a school building. It is common in other states to impose an impact fee on new residential development to secure funds to pay for new schools needed to serve the children in the new neighborhood. While a properly calculated school impact fee is constitutional, there is no general statutory authority for school impact fees in North Carolina, so they cannot be imposed.[9]

First Amendment

The First Amendment guarantees all persons important rights—freedom of religion, of speech, and of the press; the right to assemble peaceably; and the right to petition the government. Local governments must be very careful when establishing land use regulations, as the courts will invalidate zoning restrictions that even have the potential for unduly restricting First Amendment rights.

Three areas of land use regulation have received particular scrutiny from the courts on First Amendment grounds. The first is regulation of the location and operation of adult businesses, such as topless bars and adult bookstores. The second is regulation of signs. The third is regulation of the location and operation of religious land uses.

Adult Entertainment

Communities are often concerned about the potential harmful impacts of adult entertainment businesses. Many have turned to development regulations to address these concerns. For example, a county may attempt to ban "adult" bookstores but allow other bookstores, a distinction clearly based on the content of the books. Or they may want to prohibit topless bars while not outlawing all bars or alcohol sales. The First Amendment defines how far a city or county can go with these restrictions.

The First Amendment freedom of speech protects sexually explicit but non-obscene speech. (Obscenity is not protected speech; it is a criminal offense addressed by criminal laws.) In this context, "speech" includes plays, movies, books, tapes, and dance. Protected speech does not include conduct, such as serving food or drink, performing massages, or the like.

The courts have ruled that special development restrictions may be applied to adult entertainment businesses, but only if the purpose of the regulation is to prevent adverse secondary impacts of the activity, as opposed to preventing the activity itself. A local government may not ban adult businesses simply because the local government concludes these businesses are morally offensive. Rather, the local government must base a restriction on consideration of such factors as preventing prostitution and other crime, preventing the spread of disease, preventing litter, or maintaining neighboring property values. It is not necessary to show a particular adult use at a particular location will cause adverse secondary impacts, as the regulations may address the overall problem, not a particular case. Cities and counties can rely on studies of adverse secondary impacts conducted in other jurisdictions, but governing boards should be careful to discuss and consider the contribution a proposed regulation would make in reducing adverse impacts in their own communities.

The courts have upheld a variety of zoning restrictions on adult businesses. For example, zoning ordinances can require that adult businesses be confined to certain zoning districts, that they be located a minimum distance from each other, and that they be located a minimum distance from other "sensitive uses," such as schools, places of worship, and residences. State law only allows one adult business or activity to be located in a single building.

A complete ban of lawful adult businesses is not allowed. When all of the restrictions on the location of adult businesses are considered, there must be a reasonable range of alternative sites left within the jurisdiction for their location. While the government does not have to act as a real estate agent to find a readily available alternative site, the city or county does need to conduct a study to assure that after its siting restrictions are imposed some sites remain within the commercial real estate market that could become available for adult businesses. North Carolina law allows neighboring communities within an interrelated geographic area to work together to identify reasonable alternative locations (as opposed to requiring each individual jurisdiction to provide sites).

In addition to these regulations on location, various operational regulations are also permissible. For example, regulations may require a minimum separation between performers and patrons; may limit hours of operation; can set minimum lighting requirements; can prohibit closed booths or viewing areas; and can set licensing requirements for owners, operators, and employees.

Signs

Most local development ordinances regulate signs, either as part of the zoning ordinance or as a separate sign ordinance. In addition to addressing traffic safety concerns, sign regulations are permissible to protect community aesthetic values.

While most would agree that a yard sign supporting a candidate for mayor is a form of speech with First Amendment protection, does the Constitution also protect a flashing sign posted by a convenience store to advertise a sale on hot dogs? Can a city limit some types of signs while allowing others?

Is Down Zoning a Taking? The *Finch* Case

When a city rezones property to a more restrictive zoning district, an action that reduces the market value of the affected property, can the property owner sue the city and recover compensation for the change in property value?

This was the question presented by a Durham case. The dispute involved a 2.6-acre parcel just south of the interchange of Interstate 85 and Hillandale Road (see the site map on page 165). In 1947 the site was originally zoned for residential use. The immediately surrounding area was subsequently built up as a predominately single-family home subdivision, with the exception of a single gas station (which was later abandoned). In 1979 Vernon Finch and some partners obtained an option to purchase this vacant property and convinced the city council to rezone this property and the adjacent abandoned gas station from residential to commercial so they could build a 100-unit motel. After the property was rezoned to commercial use, the real estate market was a bit slow, so Finch took no immediate action to build. Some five years after the property had been rezoned for commercial use, he reached an agreement with Red Roof Inn to put a motel on the site. At that time he began the process of getting city approval to construct the motel.

As a first step to getting their building plans approved, the owners requested that the city close a street on the rear of the property. The neighbors learned of this and were very concerned about a motel being built in their neighborhood. At this point several immediate neighbors and the neighborhood association asked the city to rezone the property back to its original, pre-1979, single-family residential use. The city's planning and zoning board held a public hearing on the request and recommended returning the zoning on the property to that of a residential district. Between the planning board recommendation and city council action, Finch had to decide whether to exercise the

This motel was originally proposed for the *Finch* site. It was eventually built a mile east of the site, on the other side of the interstate highway.

option to purchase the site. He decided to proceed and purchased the property for the agreed price of $165,000. A few weeks later the city council accepted the planning board recommendation and rezoned the property back to residential use. The next month Finch entered into an agreement to sell the land to Red Roof Inn for $500,000, with the sale contingent on the property being zoned to allow a motel on the site. Since the new zoning did not allow the motel, the sale fell through and Finch sued the city.

While everyone agreed at the trial that the ordinance had considerably reduced the market value of the property, there was considerable dispute about the exact impact. The owners' experts contended the land was worth only $20,000 to $25,000 if zoned for residential use, figures considerably below the half-million dollars the owner would have received if the property was zoned commercial. The city conceded the value was reduced but contended the land with the current residential zoning was worth at least $150,000. The jury ruled there was a taking but awarded no damages. However, the trial judge then ruled that the city was liable for $151,000 in damages plus more than $61,000 for the owners' legal fees.

The city appealed and when the case got to the North Carolina Supreme Court, the court overturned this judgment.[a] The court noted that the land could still be used for residences after the rezoning and this was a practical use of the property with reasonable value. Thus the court held that even though there had been a very substantial reduction in value, this as a matter of law was not an unconstitutional taking of the owner's property.

After this case was decided, events continued to unfold. The entire site remained vacant for some years, while the proposed Red Roof Inn (see the photo on page 164)

continued

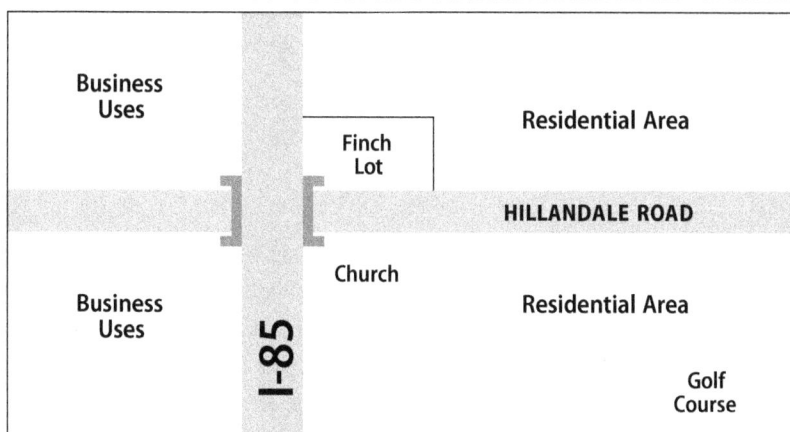

The site at issue in the *Finch* case.

was built in a commercial area a half-mile away at the next interchange. In 1993, after several additional abortive attempts to secure more intensive zoning, the owner of the part of the site where the gas station used to be requested rezoning to a low-intensity office district and submitted a site plan for an office with detailed conditions regarding a landscaped buffer, parking, and street access. This less-intrusive project had the support of the neighborhood association. The city approved the rezoning and a real estate office (see the photo below) was built on the site, a use certainly more compatible with the

This real estate office was eventually built on the property involved in the *Finch* case.

surrounding residential neighborhood than a large motel would have been. This type of practical compromise is not uncommon in zoning disputes. Thirty years after the zoning dispute, the portion of the site involved in the *Finch* litigation remains vacant.

---

a. Finch v. City of Durham, 325 N.C. 352 (1989).

The courts have held that commercial advertising is a form of speech that has some First Amendment protection. They have traditionally allowed more substantial restrictions on commercial speech, such as advertisements and billboards, than on political speech. Ordinances can ban misleading or inaccurate advertisements. Regulations can be imposed that directly advance a substantial government interest (such as promoting traffic safety or preserving community aesthetic values). Such restrictions may be no more extensive than necessary to serve that interest.

Reasonable restrictions on commercial signs are acceptable under these standards. Common regulations include limits on the size of signs, mini-

Many zoning ordinances restrict the location of adult businesses.

mum separation between signs, limits on sign illumination, limits on portable or temporary signs, prohibition of off-premise advertising, prohibition of billboards in certain zoning districts, and prohibition of all signs within a public right-of-way.

A particular First Amendment concern arises when regulations on speech are based on the content of the speech. Some typical distinctions in sign regulation are considered "content neutral" by the courts. These include distinguishing commercial from noncommercial signs. It is also considered to be content neutral to distinguish on-site from off-site messages (such as differentiating a sign identifying a business located on the same lot as the sign from a billboard advertising a product unrelated to activity on the lot where the billboard is located).

Some states and local governments have gone beyond these distinctions and adopted regulation of commercial advertising based on the content of the advertisement. For example, a city may propose to prohibit advertisement of tobacco or alcohol products near schools. The United States Supreme Court has held that, while billboard regulations to protect traffic safety and address aesthetic concerns are legitimate, any content-based restrictions on signs must be carefully and narrowly tailored to address the substantial government interest involved (such as reducing illegal underage smoking or drinking) without unduly impinging a person's ability to convey information about lawful products to adult consumers.[10]

A proliferation of advertising signs, such as these in Jacksonville, has led to sign regulation in many zoning ordinances.

Particular care is also needed when regulating noncommercial speech, especially traditional forms of political speech (such as yard signs in election season). The United States Supreme Court ruled, for example, that a city may not completely prohibit political expressions on small signs placed in the window of a person's home.[11] While reasonable restrictions are allowed (such as limits on the size of signs and how long they can be left up), particular care is needed to stay within the bounds of permissible regulation. State statutes also address regulation of political signs. These are discussed in Chapter 14.

Religious Land Uses

The First Amendment provides that government may not make a law prohibiting the free exercise of religion. The First Amendment also prohibits the establishment of a religion, which constrains how far a city or county can go in providing favorable regulatory treatment to religious uses.

These First Amendment protections can affect development regulations in several ways. The most obvious are zoning restrictions on the location of places of worship. They also affect regulations of religious places on matters such as historic district rules regarding alteration of structures, off-street parking requirements, sign regulations, and the like. A First Amendment question may also arise when development regulations are applied to related

Zoning ordinances can regulate the secular impacts of religious land uses.

activities sponsored by religious bodies, such as schools, day care centers, shelters, and soup kitchens.

The constitutional and statutory protection for free expression of religion is not an exemption from development regulation for all aspects of religious land uses. A uniform regulation of general application to secular and religious uses alike may be fully applied to religious uses.[12] However, to be valid, land use regulations of religious land uses must generally meet the following four tests:

1. The regulations must be based on secular land use impacts rather than on concern about the religious beliefs involved.[13]

2. The regulations must be applied equally to religious and secular land uses with similar impacts. For example, requirements that a church provide space for off-street parking is permissible so long as the same requirements are also applied to all other similar places of assembly.

3. The regulations must be neutrally applied to all religious uses with similar land use impacts. For example, a zoning ordinance that prohibited a mosque but allowed a church in a particular zoning district would be invalid.

4. An appropriate balance should be reached between the burdens imposed on religious practices and the resulting benefits to the governmental interests being addressed.

Congress has also enacted the Religious Land Use and Institutional-ized Persons Act (RLUIPA) to further expand protection of religious uses. RLUIPA does not attempt to exempt religious land uses from regulation, but it establishes a rule that land use regulations cannot impose a substantial burden on religious exercise (including religious assembly) unless it is in furtherance of a compelling governmental interest and is the least restrictive means of furthering that interest. It also requires religious uses to be treated on equal terms with comparable secular uses. For example, a local govern-ment could not require a place of worship to obtain a special use permit if a comparable secular use on the same site would be a permitted use without such a special permit.

The cases interpreting RLUIPA have focused on defining what constitutes a substantial burden. The courts have generally held that typical land use regulations, such as requiring provision of adequate parking, excluding reli-gious uses from small commercial areas, or requiring large religious facilities to be located in districts that allow other such intensive uses, do not impose a substantial burden.

Notes

1. San Diego Gas & Elec. Co. v. San Diego, 450 U.S. 621, 661, n.26 (Brennan, J., dissenting).

2. Discovery Network, Inc. v. City of Cincinnati, 507 U.S. 410 (1993).

3. Pa. Coal v. Mahon, 260 U.S. 393 (1922).

4. Kaiser Aetna v. United States, 444 U.S. 164 (1979); Loretto v. Teleprompter Manhattan CATV Corp., 458 U.S. 419 (1982).

5. Lucas v. S.C. Coastal Council, 505 U.S. 1003 (1992).

6. Penn Central Transp. Co. v. New York, 438 U.S. 104 (1978).

7. State v. Joyner, 286 N.C. 366, *appeal dismissed*, 422 U.S. 1002 (1975).

8. Nollan v. Cal. Coastal Comm'n, 483 U.S. 825 (1987); Dolan v. City of Tigard, 512 U.S. 374 (1994).

9. Lanvale Properties, LLC v. Cnty. of Cabarrus, 366 N.C. 142 (2012). Several North Carolina counties have special legislative authority for school impact fees.

10. Lorillard Tobacco Co. v. Reilly, 533 U.S. 525 (2001).

11. City of Ladue v. Gilleo, 512 U.S. 43 (1994).

12. Emp't Div./Dep't of Human Resources v. Smith, 494 U.S. 872 (1990).

13. Church of the Lukumi Babalu Aye, Inc. v. City of Hialeah, 508 U.S. 520 (1993).

Appendix

Selected Additional References on Land Use Law

North Carolina Materials

Statutes

The North Carolina General Statutes (hereinafter G.S.) are online at: http://www.ncleg.net/gascripts/Statutes/statutestoc.pl.

For municipalities, planning and development statutes are set out as Article 19, Chapter 160A (G.S. 160A-360 to G.S. 160A-459.1).

For counties, planning and development statutes are set out as Article 18, Chapter 153A (G.S. 153A-320 to G.S. 153A-378).

Book

Owens, David W. *Land Use Law in North Carolina.* 2d ed. Chapel Hill, N.C.: School of Government, 2011.

> 530 pages. A detailed review of the legal aspects of zoning and other land use ordinances. It covers zoning hearings, notice, protest petitions, spot and contract zoning, vested rights, nonconformities, special and conditional use permits, variances, appeals, constitutional limitations, statutory limits on zoning, and judicial review. It includes digests of all North Carolina appellate court decisions on zoning.

Reports

For free online versions or to purchase print versions of these reports, visit http://shopping.netsuite.com/s.nl/c.433425/sc.7/.f?search=special+series.

Owens, David W. *Development Moratoria: The Law and Practice in North Carolina.* Special Series No. 26, Dec. 2009. Chapel Hill, N.C.: School of Government.

28 pages. A review of the statutes and case law on the use of development moratoria. It also reports a survey of how North Carolina cities and counties have used this tool.

Owens, David W. *The North Carolina Experience with Municipal Extraterritorial Planning Jurisdiction.* Special Series No. 20, Jan. 2006. Chapel Hill, N.C.: School of Government.

17 pages. A detailed review of the legal authority for extraterritorial planning and regulatory jurisdiction. It also includes reports on how many North Carolina cities exercise this authority, the types of regulations applied in this area, the relationship of ETJ to annexation, and county policies on granting approval for municipal ETJ.

Owens, David W. *Special Use Permits in North Carolina Zoning.* Special Series No. 22, Apr. 2007. Chapel Hill, N.C.: School of Government.

28 pages. A detailed review of the legal authority for use of special and conditional use permits. It also reports a survey of how North Carolina cities and counties administer these permits.

Owens, David W. *The Use of Development Agreements to Manage Large-Scale Development: The Law and Practice in North Carolina.* Special Series No. 25, Oct. 2009. Chapel Hill, N.C.: School of Government.

28 pages. A detailed review of the legal authority for law on development agreements. It also reports a survey of how North Carolina cities and counties used this management tool in the initial few years it was available in the state.

Owens, David W. *Zoning Amendments in North Carolina.* Special Series No. 24, Feb. 2008. Chapel Hill, N.C.: School of Government.

24 pages. A detailed review of the legal issues related to zoning text and map amendments. It also reports a survey of how North Carolina cities and counties administer the zoning amendment process.

Owens, David W., and Nathan Branscome. *An Inventory of Local Government Land Use Ordinances in North Carolina.* Special Series No. 21, Apr. 2006. Chapel Hill, N.C.: School of Government.

31 pages. A report of a survey about which land use and related ordinances have been adopted by North Carolina cities and counties. It includes a brief description of the types of ordinances and a summary of the adoption rate. It also includes tables showing the status of ordinance adoption in each responding jurisdiction.

Owens, David W., and Adam Bruggemann. *A Survey of Experience with Zoning Variances.* Special Series No. 18, Feb. 2004. Chapel Hill, N.C.: School of Government.

35 pages. A detailed review of the legal authority for granting variances and judicial limitations on its use and a report on how the tool has been used in North Carolina.

Owens, David W., and Andrew Stevenson. *An Overview of Zoning Districts, Design Standards, and Traditional Neighborhood Design in North Carolina Zoning Ordinances.* Special Series No. 23, Oct. 2007. Chapel Hill, N.C.: School of Government.

28 pages. A report on a survey of the types of zoning districts included in North Carolina zoning ordinances, design standards in these ordinances, and the regulation of traditional neighborhood design (or New Urbanism) options.

Websites

Coates Canons: http://canons.sog.unc.edu

A School of Government blog on local government law, including monthly posts on planning and development regulation topics.

NC Planning: http://www.sog.unc.edu/organizations/planning

A website maintained by the School of Government. Contains links to electronic publications, legislative updates, and short courses; links to many planning sites; and frequently asked questions about land use law.

NCAPA: http://www.nc-apa.org

A website maintained by the state chapter of the professional organization for planners, the North Carolina Chapter of the American

Planning Association. Contains planning news and links to information on legislation and other planning reference material.

NCAZO: http://www.ncazo.org

A website maintained by the state's organization of city and county zoning staff, the North Carolina Association of Zoning Officials. Contains news and information on conferences and workshops on zoning issues.

Other Resources

Babcock, Richard F. *The Zoning Game: Municipal Practices and Policies.* Madison: University of Wisconsin Press, 1966.

A classic and highly readable review of the actual practice of zoning around the country, written by the preeminent land use lawyer of the time.

Dale, C. Gregory, Benjamin Herman, and Anne McBride. *The Planning Commissioners Guide.* Chicago: American Planning Association, 2013.

A popular citizens' guide to land use planning.

Juergensmeyer, Julian C., and Thomas E. Roberts. *Land Use Planning and Development Regulation Law.* 3rd ed. Eagan, MN: West Academic Publishing, 2013.

A basic single-volume treatise on zoning law in the United States.

Mandelker, Daniel R. *Land Use Law.* 5th ed. Charlottesville, VA: Lexis Law Publishing, 2003.

A basic single-volume treatise on zoning law in the United States.

Platt, Rutherford H. *Land Use and Society: Geography, Law, and Public Policy.* Washington, DC: Island Press, 2004.

A readable overview of land use planning and related public policy issues.

Toll, Seymour I. *Zoned American.* New York: Grossman, 1969.

A detailed review of the development and evolution of zoning in the United States, with a particular emphasis on the origins and early development of zoning.

Glossary

This glossary defines a number of terms that are often used in zoning and development regulation. The definitions are meant to assist the lay reader rather than being complete legal definitions.

amortization—The practice of requiring a land use or structure to come into compliance with a newly enacted regulation at the end of a specified grace period. For example, a newly enacted sign regulation could provide that if a preexisting sign is larger than allowed by a new ordinance, it may remain in place for three years, but then must be brought into compliance.

board of adjustment—A committee of citizens appointed by the city council or board of county commissioners to hear quasi-judicial zoning matters, most commonly variance petitions. The board must have at least five members and each member is appointed to a three-year term.

building permit—A permit required prior to the initiation of construction of a structure. It verifies that the proposed building's plans comply with the state building code. Many cities and counties require verification of zoning compliance before a building permit is issued.

comprehensive plan—A plan prepared by cities and counties to identify and analyze land use, development, and other issues facing the community. The plan typically is based on substantial data collection and analysis and extensive public participation and considers the interrelationships between land uses, transportation, utilities, and other public services and needs. These plans often focus on physical development and have a long-term focus (typically ten to twenty years). They are not legally mandated in

North Carolina. Although required to be considered in zoning decisions, they do not have binding legal effect.

conditional use permit—A permit required for a use that is allowed in a particular zoning district only if conditions specified in the zoning ordinance are met. A formal evidentiary hearing is required to determine if the conditions are met. Synonymous with the term "special use permit."

conditional zoning—A zoning map amendment that adds site-specific standards and conditions to the rezoning. If the rezoning also requires a concurrent conditional use permit, it is called conditional use district zoning; if the decision is entirely legislative and does not require a conditional use permit, it is called conditional zoning.

contract zoning—A situation where a city or county zones property in a requested fashion in return for promises made by the petitioner. For example, a city agrees to zone a parcel for commercial use in return for a promise by the owner to build a new city hall. Contract zoning based on such a quid pro quo is always illegal in North Carolina.

conventional zoning—A zoning district that includes a list of permitted uses and may also include uses allowed only by special or conditional use permit. It does not, however, include any standards or conditions that are applied only to individual properties.

entitlement—A permit or other mandatory regulatory approval that authorizes a specific project or development.

evidentiary hearing—The formal hearing required to gather evidence prior to making a quasi-judicial zoning decision. All of the essential elements of a fair trial must be observed, such as having witnesses under oath and subject to cross-examination; no gathering of evidence outside the hearing; written findings of fact; and substantial, competent, and material evidence in the record to support the findings.

ex parte communication—Gathering evidence or information outside the bounds of an evidentiary hearing, such as discussing a case with an applicant or staff member prior to the hearing. This is improper in quasi-judicial matters.

exaction—A requirement that an applicant provide land, construct improvements, or pay a fee as a condition of development approval. Exactions are legal so long as they are explicitly authorized by statute, are reasonably related to addressing the impacts generated by the proposed development, and are no greater in size than those roughly proportional to those impacts.

extraterritorial jurisdiction—The authority of a city to apply its planning and development regulations to a perimeter area outside of the city limits. Cities in North Carolina generally have the authority to do this in an area immediately adjacent to the city, with the size of the area varying up to three miles depending on the population of the city. This area is often referred to as the ETJ.

floating zone—Zoning districts that are defined in the zoning ordinance but that are not actually applied unless a landowner makes a request for it. An example would be a mobile home park district that is applied to property only upon the owner's request.

governing board—The elected officials responsible for adopting and amending zoning ordinances. This is the county board of commissioners or the city council (which also may be known as the village or town council or board of aldermen).

legislative hearing—A hearing held for the purpose of soliciting public comments on a proposed change in a development regulation, such as a zoning ordinance text or zoning map amendment. Reasonable time limits on speakers may be imposed and responsible decorum should be maintained. However, unlike quasi-judicial hearings, there is no requirement for oaths, no limits on expression of personal opinions, and no limit on discussing the matter outside the context of the hearing.

nonconformity—A lot, structure, or land use that is inconsistent with current development regulations but which was entirely lawful when it was originally established.

notice—The formal legal notification of a public hearing on a proposed zoning amendment or permit. A "published notice" is one required to be printed in a newspaper. A "mailed notice" is one delivered to specified individuals (usually the applicant and immediate neighbors) by U.S. mail. A "posted notice" is a temporary sign advertising a hearing that is placed on or adjacent to the property affected by the action subject to the hearing. "Actual notice" requires personal delivery of the hearing notice to the recipient.

overlay district—A zoning district that applies development standards in addition to the requirements of the basic (or "underlying") zoning district. For example, a flood plain overlay district may impose restrictions on development in flood hazard areas that are in addition to whatever requirements are imposed by the underlying residential or commercial zoning district.

permitted use—A use that is automatically approved in a zoning district. For example, a residential zoning district may list single-family homes, places of worship, and schools as permitted uses. These are also sometimes referred to as a use by right.

planning board—A citizen committee appointed by the governing board to assist in the land use planning and zoning process. The planning board reviews all proposed zoning amendments and makes a recommendation to the governing board regarding their adoption. The planning board may also be assigned some or all of the duties of the board of adjustment, most typically deciding special or conditional use permit applications.

preemption—A situation where state or federal laws cover a subject to the exclusion of local regulation.

protest petition—A formal written objection to a zoning change filed by the property owners most directly affected by the proposed amendment. If a qualifying petition is filed at least two working days prior to the day of the public hearing on a proposed zoning amendment, the amendment can only be adopted if approved by a three-fourths majority of the governing board.

quasi-judicial decisions—Those zoning decisions that require the finding of facts and the application of standards that involve judgment and discretion. Examples include special and conditional use permits and variances.

rezoning—The amendment of a zoning map to move property from one zoning district to another district.

setback—A requirement that a structure be located a minimum specified distance from a property line or other reference point. For example, a 10-foot side yard setback means a building in that district must be located at least 10 feet from the property line along the side of the lot.

special use permit—A permit required for a use that is allowed in a particular zoning district only if conditions specified in the zoning ordinance are met. A formal evidentiary hearing is required to determine if the conditions are met. This is synonymous with a conditional use permit.

spot zoning—The zoning of a relatively small area of land differently from the way the majority of the surrounding land is zoned. Spot zoning is legal only if the government establishes that it is reasonable. Reasonableness is determined by considering the size of the area; any special conditions or factors regarding the area; the consistency of the zoning with the land use plan; the degree of change in the zoning; the degree it allows uses different from the surrounding area; and the relative benefits and detriments for the owner, the neighbors, and the surrounding community.

taking—When a regulation so significantly affects the use of private property that it has the same effect as government seizure of the property. It is unconstitutional unless compensation is paid to the owner. A regulation is generally only deemed a taking if it renders the property totally valueless, it authorizes a physical invasion of the property, or the property is left with no practical use that has reasonable economic value. A reduction of property value as a result of a land use regulation is not a taking in and of itself.

UDO—A Unified Development Ordinance, which is a single ordinance that combines all of a jurisdiction's development regulations into one comprehensive ordinance. This allows a common set of definitions, boards, and procedures to be used for zoning, subdivision regulation, sign ordinance, and other types of development regulations. They are allowed but not required in North Carolina.

variance—An authorization to do something contrary to the strict terms of a zoning ordinance, such as building a structure inside a required setback area. Variances are quasi-judicial decisions that require an evidentiary hearing. They may be issued only upon a finding of unnecessary hardships as a result of strict compliance and that the variance would be consistent with the spirit, purpose, and intent of the ordinance. Variance petitions are usually assigned to the board of adjustment for hearing and decision.

vested right—The right to complete or continue development in accordance with the development rules that were in place when the right "vested" rather than having to comply with changed zoning requirements.

Index

D

dedication, 55
delays in enforcement, 75
delegation of state authority, 3–4
delivery of written decisions, 106
demolition in historic districts, 58
design standards, 51
development agreements, 140–141
dimensional standards in zoning, 47–49
dispute resolution, alternative forms of, 129
down zoning, 164–165
due process, 156–158
Durham, City of, Finch v., 164

E

Elizabeth City v. Aydlett, 36–39
enforcement, 70–75
    delays in, 75
    notices of violation, 71
    orders to demolish, 75
    orders to repair, 75
    stop work orders, 71
enforcement actions, 69
equal protection, 158–159
evidence
    burden of producing, 99, 120
    opinion, 103–104
evidentiary hearings, 9, 97–104, 138
exactions, 63, 161
ex parte communication, 104
extraterritorial area, 146
extraterritorial jurisdiction (ETJ), 13, 15–22
    boards of adjustment and, 21
    boundary map hearings, 20

F

Fair Housing Act, 148
family care homes, 147–148
farms, bona fide, 146
fees, 62, 69–70, 79
final plats, 55
Finch v. City of Durham, 164–166
findings, 107
First Amendment, 162–170